Standing tall against the bright sky of Guanajuato, Mexico, is an unusual church called "La Valenciana." The town, one of the most beautiful in Mexico, was built over incredibly rich deposits of silver and gold. So rich were some of the citizens of Guanajuato that it was not unusual for them to throw silver dust in the path of a wedding procession! It is said that at one point during the building of the church of La Valenciana, the supply of mortar ran out. What to do? How could the stones stand strong without mortar? In Guanajuato, the answer was easy. There was plenty of silver and plenty of wine . . . so much of each that silver dust and Spanish wine were used as mortar; the work went on. So our story goes . . .

by Joan and Gene Olson

SILVER DUST AND SPANISH WINE:
A History of Mexico

WINDYRIDGE PRESS

ISBN 0-913366-06-4
LC 80-51869

Published by:
WINDYRIDGE PRESS
P. O. Box 591
Rogue River, Oregon 97537

Printed in the United States of America

972
OL8s
118099
May 1981

PHOTO CREDITS

ACKNOWLEDGMENTS

Most prominent among those in the United States and Mexico who helped with this book are the following:

Frank and Shirley Arnich; Adolfo Baqueiro S., Mérida; Daniel Bazán, University of Texas Institute of Texan Cultures; Laura Simmons Bullion, University of Texas Institute of Texan Cultures; Barbara Bush, Arizona Historical Society; Rudolph Casavantes, Chihuahua; Martin Cole; Joe Coltharp, University of Texas Humanities Research Center Library; Katherine DeJarnett; Pam de Loetz; Harvey Dickey; T. R. Fehrenbach; Roy L. Flukinger, University of Texas Humanities Research Center Library; Laura Gálvez Ortiz, Mexico City; Mary Garcia, New Mexico Dept. of Education; Alfonso Guadarrama, Mexico City; Andrew Gutiérrez; Elisa De Leon Gutierrez, Texas Dept. of Education; Frances Alderete de Gutiérrez; Manuel Hernández R., Guanajuato; Lic. Arturo Herrera Cabañas, Archivo Fotografico Casasola, Pachuca; Alice Holmes, Arizona State Museum; Alice L. Johnson, San Antonio Conservation Society; Chela Kocks, Southern Oregon State College; May Ellen MacNamara, University of Texas Humanities Research Center Library; Jack Maguire, University of Texas Institute of Texan Cultures; Henry Mattison, a gringo friend-in-need in Mexico City; Catherine McDowell, The Library, Daughters of the Republic of Texas; Lic. Javier Oropeza y Segura, Instituto Nacional de Antropologia e Historia, Mexico City; Arthur L. Olivas, Museum of New Mexico; Henry Pascual, New Mexico Dept. of Education; Augustín Pérez V., the best taxi driver and cigar maker in all of Puebla; Noe Ramos Limón, Tehuacan; Robert Revilla; Con Sellers; Conrad True, San Antonio Conservation Society; Kenneth C. Turner, Library, Organization of American States; Polo Vargas, Guadalajara; Angelle Warneke, El Paso Public Library; Shirley Watson, El Paso Public Library; Maria Watson, Library, Daughters of the Republic of Texas; Bert Webber; Dorothy Yancy, Arizona Dept. of Education.

Thank you all.

CONTENTS

"Poor Mexico! So far from God, so close to
the United States." - - - Anonymous

THE SHOUT OF DOLORES

Long live the independence of Mexico!
Long live Hidalgo!
Long live Morelos!
Long live the heroes who gave us our country and liberty!
Long live Mexico!
Long live Mexico!
Long live Mexico!

ONE

--- The Ancient Ones

"THE MOST BEAUTIFUL CITY IN THE WORLD . . . "

They were called *conquistadores*, or "conquerors." They had come from Cuba, only a short distance away. But they were not Cuban; they were Spanish.

With their horses and armor and cannon, they had entered the mysterious new land from the east. After sweating through coastal swamps and struggling over mountain passes higher than any they had seen before, they stopped and stared in wonder.

One of them, a soldier named Bernal Díaz del Castillo, described the scene in his journal: "We were amazed, and we said it was like the enchantments they tell of in the legend of Amadis, on account of the great towers, and temples and buildings rising from the water, and all built of masonry. And some of our soldiers even asked whether the things that we saw were not a dream. . .seeing things as we did that had never been heard of or seen before, not even dreamed about."

The slope trailed off to an enormous lake. Small boats painted in brilliant colors coasted over the quiet waters, sliding in and out of the morning mists. Ribbons of earth and rock and masonry connected the shoreline to an island. It was this island which drew their eyes.

For on the island was a city of a size and color and magnificence never seen before by these much-travelled men. Nor even imagined. . .

Díaz wrote: "I say again that. . . never in the world would there be discovered other lands such as these. . . "

The expedition's leader, Hernán Cortés, stated his feeling in a letter to his emperor in Spain: "The most beautiful city in the world. . ."

The city was Tenochtitlán, center of the Aztec empire. It was in the heart of what is now called Mexico. The year was 1519.

Small wonder that Díaz and Cortés were impressed. In 1519, the great Aztec city had a population of 250,000, five times larger than the London of that day. Tenochtitlán was even more beautiful than Venice, glittering crown jewel of Europe.

And so it happened on a misty morning in 1519 that the eyes of some Europeans were opened. They discovered that there was more in the world beyond the seas than savages and plunder.

When Cortés and Díaz first laid startled eyes on it, Tenochtitlán had existed for less than 200 years, a mere tick of history's clock. In this enormous Valley of Mexico and beyond, generation had followed generation in a great ebb and flow of human history.

Then a member of a wandering tribe, perhaps footsore and weary, did a remarkable thing: he tamed a wild plant called maize and became the world's first corn farmer. No longer did he have to take what food nature chose to provide; he could plant and harvest his own; he could settle down by the side of the road.

It should not be assumed that everybody in the neighborhood promptly dropped spears and picked up hoes. Modern humans think of time as a rushing stream and of themselves as bobbing corks on the water. But in ancient days, change came slowly, naturally, like wind wearing away rock. Almost 4000 years passed before farmers turned to the building of cities.

The first ears of corn were pretty pitiful, not much larger than a cigarette filter; fossilized remains have been found. But improvement followed improvement, until at last wanderers could be farmers. They no longer had to live in brush huts at the mercy of the wild food supply, forced to move on to greener pastures when hunger gnawed. Irrigation of the maize fields followed; dry earth was turned into rich cropland. Thus a blow was struck against another old enemy of man --- drought.

Now stable societies could be formed. Permanent houses could be built, then markets and temples. Farmers turned into city-builders. Artists and weavers and craftsmen of all kinds appeared, along with merchants and priests and even politicians.

A long step had been taken toward what we like to call civilization. A few more ticks of time --- about 6000 years --- and there would arise the marvelous city called Tenochtitlán to dazzle the eyes of the intruding Spaniards.

And then it would end and the glory would die.

What happened during those 6000 years?

Everything happened. The pageant of human history was presented in bright colors under a brilliant Mexican sun. Tribes formed nations and swallowed up other nations, then in turn were swallowed up. Some nations reached out and were destroyed by their own ambitions; others lurked in the shadows and worked at their arts and crafts, only to be destroyed when the warlike ones thundered into their secret places. Winners made slaves out of losers, then were in turn enslaved. Wild and bloody religions flourished, then fell out of favor. Governments formed, governments collapsed. Enormous structures rose to gleam in many colors against the hard blue skyline, buildings which modern man has yet to match. Brilliant work was done in science, in writing, in art, in government.

Great stone heads like these were found at La Venta, in the state of Tabasco. The interesting Negroid features and football helmet are typical. Many of these heads are in La Venta Park, near Villahermosa, not far from where they were found. This particular sculpture is in Mexico City at the Museum of Anthropology.

The names are strange, difficult to pronounce, even more difficult to remember: Olmec... Teotihuacán... Zapotec... Huasteca... Chichimec...

Many of these strange-sounding words, pronounced as if they were Spanish, are scattered over maps of modern Mexico, adding interest to geography and confusion to tourists.

The Olmec culture is considered to be mother and father to the others. Think of Olmec and you should think of jaguars, because this handsome cat was their major symbol. Thinking Olmec, one must also think of their enormous stone sculpture, with helmeted heads, wide noses and thick lips. A fair amount of this startling stuff is still lying around in Mexico.

ANCIENT EGGHEADS

A fairly late-blooming culture was that of the Mayan people. (In fact, they were so far advanced that their name is even easy to spell and pronounce.) One might consider Mayans the eggheads of ancient Mexico.

Mayan country was a vast area centering on the Yucatán peninsula, which contains the modern Mexican states of Chiapas, Campeche and Tabasco and the territory of Quintana Roo. But Mayans stretched their influence into parts of Central America, too.

So what was so great about the Mayans? Listen:

At a time when much of the world's population was trying to figure out a better way to barbecue squirrels, Mayans in Mexico were developing calendars more accurate than the one we use today. They also built astronomical observatories; they designed buildings more beautiful than most modern ones; they developed a very sophisticated form of hieroglyphic (picture) writing.

Then in their spare time, Mayans came up with the mathematical idea of "zero" long before the idea was used in Europe. (About that zero business --- mathematicians seem to consider this very important, even though it may seem like nothing to the rest of us.)

In the Mayan cities, many peculiar pillars were built. Engraved on them were dates and brief accounts of major news

This is how some Mayan skeletons were found. The graves are recreated in the Museum of Anthropology, Mexico City.

events. "Stelae," we call them. The balance and beauty of stelae and of figures carved into their temples have led some experts to call Mayans the greatest artists yet produced by the human race.

A TOMB OF GOLD

On January 9, 1932, a party of archaeologists (students of ancient things) led by Dr. Alfonso Caso was poking around a graveyard on a mountaintop. They were near Oaxaca, a lovely little city in the south of Mexico.

Their discoveries on that day were to cause them to go without sleep for the next seven days. Tomb 7, Monte Albán, was about to be laid bare. For the next seven days and seven nights, the archaeologists excitedly scratched their way into the tomb.

Each new find seemed to outshine the last --- masks of solid gold, exquisitely worked jade, polished crystal ornaments, turquoise mosaics of brilliant beauty, gold breast-plates, pendants of gold carved with great delicacy, strings of huge pearls, necklaces of turquoise and gold, vases of alabaster glowing with ghostly light.

Monte Albán, for centuries a ceremonial center and burial ground for the Mixtec and Zapotec peoples, remains one of Mexico's most breathtaking archaeological sites. In the valley below, Oaxaca draws a constant stream of visitors because of a museum next door to the famous church of Santo Domingo. Here, displayed under soft light, glows some of the Tomb 7 treasure.

AVENUE OF THE DEAD

"Teotihuacán" --- it is hard to say. Once seen, Teotihuacán is hard to forget. This huge complex of restored ruins 19 kilometers northeast of Mexico City has often been called the most spectacular sight in Mexico. Pawed over by archaeologists for decades, it remains a place of mystery.

The name means "Place of the Gods." There is much evidence to indicate that it was the first large city in Middle America (Mexico and Central America).

An old man, Chinese perhaps? Interesting thought, that, because this ancient figure in the Museum of Anthropology, Mexico City, was found in the state of Veracruz.

Hernán Cortés passed through the valley below this site without discovering its riches. These are the old temples on a mountain-top, Monte Albán near Oaxaca, before restoration was begun.

Teotihuacán has three major features: Pyramid of the Moon, Pyramid of the Sun and Temple of Quetzalcóatl. Connecting these is a three-kilometer thoroughfare called "Avenue of the Dead."

One gigantic object along the avenue dominates all others ---Pyramid of the Sun. Two hundred and fourteen meters square at its base and 20 stories tall, this enormous structure is made of earth, sun-dried bricks and stone. It is one of the largest human-built objects in the world.

The Mexican government has spent millions to restore Teotihuacán as a historical showcase and major tourist attraction. Teotihuacán of today is a place of massive shapes and pleasing lines dappled with interesting shadows, but with little color. It was not always so.

When Teotihuacán was in its glory, it gladdened the eye with glowing tones of red and blue and yellow. In the clean air of old Mexico, Teotihuacán in living color must have been a sight to take one's breath away. The Museum of Anthropology in Mexico City displays a replica of a section of temple wall in what may be the original colors; it is one of the most striking exhibits in this world-famous museum.

But what of the mystery of Teotihuacán, you ask?

Just this: nobody knows who these talented people were, where they came from or exactly what happened to them and their beautiful city. They came from somewhere, they lived and built, then disappeared. For seven centuries, they spread their culture over Middle America; then, somehow, Teotihuacán died. Why? Archaeologists are still guessing.

There are actually two Teotihuacáns, one built over the ruins of the other. This happened again and again in Mexico. At Cholula, about 96 kilometers southeast of Mexico City, there is a pyramid which is even larger at its base than the Pyramid of the Sun, but not so tall. The Cholula pyramid is not just one, but seven pyramids, built one on top of another!

Compared to Pyramid of the Sun, the Cholula mass is not impressive at first glance. Because much of it is yet to be restored, it has a scruffy look. But Cholula draws many visitors because of a startling feature: one can go deep inside, through all seven pyramids; one can stroll along exploration tunnels to inspect ancient art on the dark, clammy walls. Archaeologists puzzled over Cholula for many years; now they think it was part of the Teotihuacán culture.

TOUGH AS A TOLTEC

Think of "Toltec" and one must think of warrior.

Some of the arts and skills of the Teotihuacán people rubbed off on the Toltecs but not enough to kill the appeal of their bloodthirsty gods. "Bloodthirsty" is the right word, too. Part of the Toltec religious practice (and also of the Aztecs who came along later) was to take sacrificial victims to temples atop the pyramids, where priests would cut their hearts out.

The bloody, still-beating hearts were then offered to the gods.

When we sit in reclining chairs today and read of victims being led to the altar, it is easy to imagine protesting screams. But it may not have been like this at all when Toltecs and Aztecs conducted their bloody fiestas.

The Toltecs, for instance, seemed to make war on neighboring city-states for no better reason than to take prisoners for sacrifices to their gods. But often the captives were warriors. To them, a ceremonial death as a sacrifice to a warrior-god was not a bad way to go. It was a means of entry into that glorious Old Soldiers' Home in the Sky.

There surely were a few who grumbled, "This is an honor I could do without." But the thing to remember is that human sacrifice in those days was not capital punishment, nor was it simple extermination. It was religious ritual which may have served a useful purpose. population control.

Toltecs ranged far and wide from their capital city of Tullan, conquering vast areas and many peoples. But exactly where was majestic Tullan? For many years, archaeologists tried to track it down and failed. Tullan was a ghost town, lost in one of history's dark places.

Only recently, archaeologists decided that a place called Tula, 80 kilometers north of Mexico City, probably was the site

The grand sweep of Teotihuacán is seen from the Pyramid of the Moon. Avenue of the Dead reaches into the distance. At left center is the monster, Pyramid of the Sun. Teotihuacán, near Mexico City, has seen more restoration work than any other Mexican archaeological site.

At the lost city, Tula, one sees these dramatic figures, which once were temple columns. White dust on figures does not indicate great age; it indicates cement factories in the modern Tula Valley.

they were looking for. Work on the ruins is moving ahead rapidly, for Tula is now thought of as one of the most important historic sites in the entire country. From Tula spread the culture which dominated most of Middle America until the Spanish knocked on the door in 1519.

Tullan will be a ghost town no longer.

THE EAGLE AND THE SERPENT

Their gods had told them, "You will see an eagle perched upon a cactus. The eagle will be eating a snake. This is the place for you to settle."

Or so their priests said. . .

They were a small tribe of hungry wanderers called "Mexica." On one fine day in June, 1325, they saw the eagle on a barren island in a great lake. Here they founded the city of Tenochtitlán, which would one day become Mexico City, capital of modern Mexico and one of the largest cities in the world. The flag and seal of Mexico still bear the symbol of the eagle and serpent. The name "Mexico" comes from Mexica.

The ancestors of the starving people who founded Tenochtitlán had come from a place they called "Aztlan;" thus the people came to be known as Aztecs. As Aztecs they would rule, then write the last wild chapter of Mexican Indian history.

What about that neat little eagle-serpent legend? Well, there are those who think that Mexica priests saw that it would be smart for a weak tribe to live on an island. So they came up with the eagle-serpent yarn and sold it to their followers. True or not, it worked. The Aztec empire was off and roaring.

FLOATING FOOD

In between wars, Aztecs had some peaceful ideas. One of their best was the *chinampa*, or floating garden. *Chinampas* came about when hungry Aztecs discovered that they could cut canals through the marsh around their little island and pile vegetation between retaining walls. Then they piled earth on top of the vegetation to make plots of fertile farmland. This one little trick may have saved the Aztec empire.

No longer were the Aztecs dependent on mainland peoples for food. No longer did they have to fear being cut off by an enemy and starved out of their island fortress.

There is evidence that *chinampas* served another purpose. Once the people of Tenochtitlán wanted to send a gift to a mainland town. So they cut loose a *chinampa* bearing ripe grain, fruit and egg-laying ducks. Then they floated it across the lake to the town! Message: "You don't have to feed us any more. We ll feed you. . . if we feel like it."

GOD? MAN? OR BOTH?

The name is hard to pronounce, almost impossible to spell: "Quetzalcóatl." Say it: "ket-sahl-COH-atl."

And mark it well, for the name rattles around in ancient Mexican history like a bolt in a bucket. Quetzalcóatl was a god, not a bloodthirsty one but a nice god who controlled things like stars and winds and growing plants. His symbol was a snake wearing feathers. When nice gods were in favor, Quetzalcóatl was just about everybody's favorite.

Some believed that he was light-skinned and bearded and that he had come from across the sea. Sounds harmless, doesn't it?

Well, there is a strong feeling among historians that this belief, combined with a fantastic coincidence of the calendar, destroyed the last great Mexican Indian culture and forced the tender neck of Mexico under a Spanish boot for almost three centuries.

How could such a thing happen?

To start with, nice gods fell out of favor. The Toltecs were warlike, remember? No nice gods for them; blood and guts was the name of their game.

Things would have been a good deal more simple if Quetzalcóatl had remained a god, nice or not. But one of his admirers, a rising young Toltec named Topiltzin, decided that while his monicker had a fine ring to it, something was missing. So he added the name "Quetzalcóatl."

What he added to history was confusion. Now there was a god, Quetzalcóatl, known far and wide as the carrier of knowledge and civilization. There was also a man, Quetzalcóatl, who became king of the Toltecs and turned Tullan (Tula) into a great city and brought culture to its people.

This is El Castillo, at Chichén Itzá in Yucatán, before repair work was begun.

But warlike Toltecs had other ideas. Quetzalcóatl, both god and man, seemed pretty sissified to them. Their tastes ran to a god like Tezcatlipoca, who devoured still-beating hearts and drank warm human blood.

Nice gods don't always lose but Quetzalcóatl (the man) lost this one.

One fine evening, as the story goes, Tezcatlipoca put on the disguise of an old man. Then he proceeded to get Topiltzin Quetzalcóatl drunk.

On the morning after, Quetzalcóatl suffered so much from his hangover that he quit the Toltec throne and went into exile.

One version of the story is that Quetzalcóatl (the man) sailed out into the ocean aboard a raft made of entwined snakes. As he departed, he swore that he would return one day to rule Mexico.

This is El Castillo at Chichén Itzá after restoration. Not huge, this pyramid, but just plain handsome.

Told and retold, the stories drifted through the mists of time. The stories became legend; it would be this legend which would help to deliver Mexico into the hands of a foreign conqueror.

Some historians say they have all sorts of evidence that Quetzalcóatl (the god) wasn't a god at all; he was a real person who had floated over from Asia on a bamboo raft. Others see Hebrew symbols in old Mexican stone carving and suggest that Quetzalcóatl was a European Jew.

Whatever else he might have been, he is a fascinating mystery.

TIMELESS TEMPLES OF STONE

The trail of the ancient ones through Mexico is blurred in places. In other places, the trail is sharp and hard as the Mexican sun. The old ones built mostly in stone and stone endures. The

One of the most spectacular structures at restored Teotihuacán is the temple of Quetzalcóatl. What a breathtaking sight it must have been in full color!

This is Tlaloc, god of rain. Standing upright, Tlaloc now guards the entrance to the Museum of Anthropology, Mexico City. Brought from the village of Coatlinchán, Tlaloc entered Mexico City in April after a long period of drought. Soon after Tlaloc's arrival, the city was drenched with the heaviest rainfall ever recorded in April. A stunning coincidence...surely nothing more?

record is there today, waiting for the eyes and minds of those who care, of those who wonder and try to understand. It seems likely that no other country in the world offers such a feast of ancient history. The Yucatán peninsula alone has 800 known archaeological sites, only a few of which have been studied and restored.

Teotihuacán, Monte Albán, Tula, Cholula, Palenque, Chichén Itzá, Uxmal, Mitla --- the list is long and still growing. Seeing these magnificent places, one wonders how it could have ended as it did, when it did.

Hernán Cortés, the Spaniard, appeared in Mexico during the year called "One Reed" or *Ce Acatl* on the Aztec calendar.

This may have been one of history's most fantastic flukes. Old legends foretold that in the year One Reed --- 1519 --- Quetzalcóatl would return to resume his rule.

Quetzalcóatl had a beard.

Hernán Cortés had a beard.

So our modern civilization is not the first to be upset by human hair.

TWO

--- The Spanish Conquest

OUT OF THE SUNRISE: SANTIAGO!

For a superstitious people like the Aztecs, the signs had looked bad for some time. Perhaps the strange happenings would have been less worrisome if Moctezuma II, their respected emperor for 17 years, had been able to hide his fears. But Moctezuma was disturbed, too, and his people knew it.

More than once, an old woman had been heard wailing in the dark streets, "O my beloved sons, now we are about to go!"

Unexplained fires had broken out in the sacred temples on top of the pyramids. Mysterious lights glowed over the great city, haunting the night sky, making sleep impossible for restless citizens. Worst of all, a fisherman had found a peculiar bird; he hurried to show it to his emperor.

The bird had a mirror in its head. Looking into the mirror, Moctezuma was said to have seen armed men riding on the backs of strange, four-legged creatures. In the mirror, the warriors moved confidently, like conquerors . . .

Statuary at a corner of the Zócalo in Mexico City commemorates the founding of Tenochtitlán near this very spot. Eagle eating serpent is at left; astounded Aztecs are at right. Teenagers in foreground think it's a nice place to sit. Man working at left is probably thinking: "Another day, another peso."

Fearful citizens stared at each other over warming fires in the heavy darkness. Some thought of the old Toltec legend, the tale of Quetzalcóatl, the bearded one, who had sworn to return from out of the sunrise.

"Perhaps he has already come," muttered the most fearful.

There had been stories drifting in from the east about weird "floating houses" on the water. There were also rumors of creatures whose weapons were thunder and lightning, whose bodies could not be pierced by javelins or stones, whose faces were bearded.

In the dark streets of Tenochtitlán as the year of *Ce Acatl* approached, many things went bump in the night.

DOGS FOR SUPPER

The bearded ones were there, all right, just as the rumors whispered, but they were not led by the god Quetzalcóatl. They were led by a mortal man who was about to make himself immortal.

Hernán Cortés, 35 years old in the moment of history at which we meet him, was embarked on the great adventure of his life.

Gods? Or were they human beings, with sore feet and head colds? Listen again to the soldier, Bernal Díaz:

"We slept near a stream and with the grease from a fat Indian whom we killed and cut open, we dressed our wounds, for we had no oil, and we supped very well on some dogs which the Indians breed . . ."

And this was before things really got rough.

They had sailed from Cuba knowing very little of what the new land held in store for them. After they landed, Captain Cortés ordered their ships burned. There would be no easy return to Cuba.

What great passion drove them to take such wild risks in strange lands?

The Spanish of the 16th century, under their ambitious king, Charles V, had a grand vision: there was a rich world, largely unknown in Europe, which might be reached by Spanish sailing ships, conquered by Spanish cannon and plundered of its gold and jewels.

And all of this killing and plundering could be done in the name of the Lord Jesus Christ. After all, the natives of these lands were not Christians; they were pagans given to all sorts of evil practices. God commanded that these savages be brought into the Christian fold. . . or be wiped out. Or so it seemed to the Spanish.

Hernán Cortés had appointed himself to be God's tool in Mexico. Thus he set in motion one of history's boldest campaigns of human conquest.

About to move inland, Cortés gathered his troops and said:
"We all understand what is the work that lies before us. With the help of our Lord Jesus Christ we must conquer in all battles for if we are anywhere defeated, we can not raise our heads again, as we are so few in numbers. We can look for no help or assistance but that which comes from God, for we no longer possess ships in which to return to Cuba, but must rely on our own good swords and stout hearts. . . "

In his chronicle, Díaz reported:
"Cortés ordered a count of his forces. . . and he found that there were 508, not counting shipmasters, pilots and sailors, of which there were about 100. There were 16 horses. . . There were 32 crossbowmen and 13 musketeers, and some brass guns, and four falconets and much powder and ball."

And with this tiny army, Hernán Cortés planned to sweep aside the powerful Aztec empire!

NOT ALL WERE BEARDED

A very important person in the Cortés party was a young Indian woman. It is possible that the expedition would have failed without her.

A slave, she had been given to Cortés not long after the *conquistadores* had landed. He named her "Marina" and took her on as mistress, advisor and interpreter. The Indians referred to her as "Malinche" and sometimes used the same name for Cortés. Skilled in two Indian languages and a good student of Spanish, Doña Marina was to prove invaluable.

But had Doña Marina cast her lot with one of history's out-standing idiots? It might seem so. After all, this reckless Span-iard had burned his ships behind him. Now he marched into the mountains with a few hundred men to assault an emperor who lived on a fortified island, who could call on hundreds of thou-sands of warriors to defend it!

Cortés wasn't an idiot, of course. He had learned two im-portant facts: (1) Moctezuma's empire had been hammered to-gether by brute force and most of the subject peoples hated Az-tecs with a passion; (2) Some Indians, possibly even Moctezuma himself, had heard the Quetzalcóatl legend and they might be ready to believe that Cortés was the bearded god.

These could prove to be stronger weapons than those he brought from Cuba.

It was a strange invasion during those early weeks. As the Cortés party moved inland against slight resistance, they met ambassadors sent by Moctezuma. The ambassadors greeted Cortés and gave him gifts. Artists were sent to make paintings for Moctezuma of the Spanish equipment and horses.

Cortés treated Moctezuma's people with great courtesy. Then he made a point of demonstrating the speed of the horses in a battle charge and the lightning and thunder of the cannons. Especially the cannons. . .

MEANWHILE, BACK IN TENOCHTITLAN. . .

Tendile, Aztec ambassador to Cortés, hurried to his em-peror upon returning to Tenochtitlán. With great excitement, he told Moctezuma of all the wonderful things he had seen at the camp of Cortés, then showed his ruler the pictures painted by the artists. Finally Tendile handed over the gift.

It was a soldier's metal helmet, once gilded, now rusty. Tendile had asked Cortés for it after noticing a strange thing --- it was very much like the helmet worn by the most important god of the Aztecs, Huizilopochtli.

Díaz wrote: "When the emperor examined the helmet and that which was on Huizilopochtli, he felt convinced that we be-longed to the race which, as his forefathers had foretold, would come to rule over that land."

The trap was closing on Moctezuma and the Aztec empire.

Cortés had been advised by Indians near the coast to march to Tenochtitlán via Tlaxcala, a town about 100 kilometers east of the Aztec capital. The Indians of Tlaxcala, Cortés was told, were bitter enemies of the Aztecs; they had suffered from bloody Aztec raids for more than a century.

The Spaniards were not just an invading army; they were tourists, too, and their eyes popped at some of the sights along the trail. Díaz wrote: "I remember that in the plaza where some of their temples stood, there were piles of human skulls neatly arranged so that one could count them, and I estimated them at more than one hundred thousand. I repeat; there were more than one hundred thousand of them. And in another part of the plaza there were so many piles of dead man's thigh bones that one could not count them; there was also a large number of skulls strung between beams of wood. . . "

Apparently Cortés was impressed, too. In a letter to his king, he wrote.

"Each day they burn incense in these temples and sometimes sacrifice their own persons, some cutting their tongues, others their ears, while there are some who stab their bodies with knives. All the blood which flows from them they offer to those idols sprinkling it in all parts of the temple, or sometimes throwing it into the air or performing many other ceremonies. . . They have a most horrid and abominable custom which truly ought to be punished. . . whenever they wish to ask something of the idols. . . they take many girls and boys and even adults, and in the presence of the idols they open their chests while they are still alive and take out their hearts and entrails and burn them before the idols, offering the smoke as sacrifice. Some of us have seen this, and they say it is the most terrible and frightful thing they have ever witnessed."

➡

This room in the Museum of Anthropology, Mexico City, has prime exhibits like the Aztec calendar stone at left and reproduction of Moctezuma's headdress in case at right. The headdress is made of bright green feathers.

One has to wonder why Cortés was horrified. This was the same Cortés who had told his king in another letter about troubles with unfriendly Indians near the coast. Fifty Indians had entered camp offering food and friendship but Cortés suspected they were spies. Let Cortés tell what happened next:

"Then I took five or six and they all confirmed what I had heard, so I took all 50 and cut off their hands and sent them to tell their chief that by day or by night, or whenever they chose to come, they would see who we were."

On this occasion, Cortés may have thought he was being kind. On another occasion, he cut off hands and feet of Indian prisoners. Isn't it interesting that when Cortés did these things, he considered it a Christian duty but when Indians did them, he considered it "horrid"... "abominable"... "terrible"... "frightful"?

SURPRISE AT TLAXCALA

Cortés and company crossed the Tlaxcala frontier on August 31, 1519, to be greeted with one of life's little surprises. Instead of friendly Indians eager to march on Tenochtitlán, they found thousands of fierce warriors ready to kill Spaniards.

The Spanish battle cry was *"Santiago!"* or, sometimes, *"Señor Santiago!"* referring to the apostle James, patron saint of Spain. Cortés found many opportunities to cry *"Santiago!"* during his first few days in Tlaxcala.

Cortés wanted to talk honeyed words, as only Cortés could, to win over Tlaxcala. But it was difficult to do this with Tlaxcalans throwing lances at Spaniards. Tlaxcalans had fought Aztec invaders for decades; fighting was almost automatic. (Later, in Tenochtitlán, one of the Spaniards asked Moctezuma why he had not conquered Tlaxcala. Moctezuma replied, "We could easily do so, but then there would be nowhere for the young men to exercise themselves without going a long way off, and besides we always like to have people to sacrifice to our gods.")

After a series of skirmishes and the first great battle on September 2, the Spanish army had been cut to 400 soldiers. And some of those, according to Díaz, were wounded and sick.

The Tlaxcalans attacked twice more but were beaten off. However, victory did not seem sweet to Díaz, who wrote of the morning after.

"When we awoke and saw how all of us were wounded... and how tired we were and how many were sick and clothed in rags... and already over 45 of our soldiers had been killed or died from disease and another dozen of them were ill, and our captain himself was suffering from fever... and what with our labors and the weight of our arms which we always carried on our backs and other hardships including the lack of salt, for we could never find any, we began to wonder what would be the result of all this fighting and what we should do and where we should go when it was finished. To march into Mexico we thought too hard an undertaking because of its great armies, and we said to one another that if these Tlaxcalans, which our Cempoalan friends had led us to believe were peaceful, could reduce us to this condition, what would happen when we found ourselves at war with the great forces of Moctezuma?"

Díaz might have used other words, "With friends like these, who needs enemies?"

But the worst was over for the moment. Those "Cempoalan friends" mentioned by Díaz were coastal Indians who had joined the Cortés party. They scurried around among the Tlaxcalans spreading propaganda. The Spanish were gods, said the Cempoalans; they could not be defeated in battle.

The Tlaxcalans, battered and bloody, weren't hard to convince. Now they had cause to wonder: Can even the mighty Moctezuma prevail against the likes of these?

To the enormous relief of Cortés and his sick, tired company, the Tlaxcalans decided to join up. Without the Tlaxcalans, the story would have had a different ending.

➡

"I say again that... never in the world would there be discovered other lands such as these... " Cortés and soldiers are amazed at first view of Tenochtitlán.

MASSACRE AT CHOLULA

It is conceivable that this wild idea had already occurred to Cortés as his army rested in Tlaxcala: Was it possible that he could talk his way into Tenochtitlán, that he could take over the empire of Moctezuma without firing a single shot?

Ambassadors from Moctezuma continued to appear in the Cortés camp, bearing gifts and sweet talk from their emperor. Some even offered to guide the party to Tenochtitlán and suggested a route via Cholula, only a few miles to the south. The easiest road, they said.

Tlaxcalans, who trusted Aztecs not at all, warned against the Cholula route. But Cortés chose it just the same. Then the plucky Tlaxcalans offered to send along 10,000 warriors for protection. Cortés pointed out that they were going in friendship and that 1000 warriors would do nicely, thank you.

There was a great battle at Cholula; the Spaniards won again. But the Cholula affair may have been more of a massacre than a fair fight. Some witnesses to the blood bath place the number of Indian dead as high as 10,000! Perhaps the total doesn't matter; it didn't matter to Cortés. What mattered to *El Capitán* was that he and his Spaniards, accompanied by 4000 Tlaxcalans and 400 Cempoalans, fought their way clear of Cholula and advanced on the capital of Mexico.

In Tenochtitlán, no more than 80 kilometers away as the arrow flies, the almighty emperor of the Aztecs soon learned the details of the Cholula happening. Quite possibly he shook in his golden sandals.

GREAT FORTRESS OF MEXICO

Small wonder that Cortés had no great urge to fight his way into Tenochtitlán.

Moctezuma, it was reported, could summon quickly an army of 150,000 warriors --- and this was just a start. On the frontiers of his empire were tens of thousands more. They had neither horses nor cannon, but they did have deadly javelins with sharpened stone heads, which could be propelled at killing velocity by the *atlatl*, or throwing stick. They had slingshots, bows and arrows and spears. For fighting at close quarters, they used the *macuahuitl*, a club at least three feet long set with rows of sharp stone fragments. Did it work? It was said that a *macua-huitl* could take off a horse's head with a single blow.

The Aztecs had shields of bark or cane and wore cotton armor, sometimes jacket length, sometimes ankle length. The armor was interesting; it consisted of strips of cotton soaked in brine and wound tightly around the body as many as 20 times. It was lighter and cooler than the metal armor of the Spaniards; it was adopted by some Spanish soldiers when they learned that they might have to live for weeks without daring to take off their armor, even to sleep. (Díaz mentions his annoyance at the Indian practice of spraying incense all over the Spaniards when meeting in a friendly situation. Díaz assumed it was a religious ritual but maybe not. After living in their armor for weeks in that warm climate, the Spanish must have stunk to high heaven.)

Then there was the island fortress in which these hordes of warriors could make a stand. Many Tenochtitlán houses were built over the water on pilings and *chinampas* and were connected by bridges. All of the houses, the Spaniards had been told, had flat roofs which could be walled up in case of attack.

But best of all for its defense, the city could be entered only over three causeways; these were rock and dirt ramps reaching into the lake from the mainland. The causeways weren't solid, each had four or five openings to allow water to flow from one part of the lake to another. Over each opening stretched a wooden bridge. Raise just one bridge on each causeway and the capital of Mexico was safe from invaders . . . in theory.

Díaz was impressed, but his chronicle shows his complete confidence that greed would conquer all:

"Then an Indian told of the large supplies of gold and silver and rich stones and other wealth owned by Moctezuma . . . The more he said about the great fortress and of the bridges, of such material are we Spanish soldiers made that the more we heard, the more we wanted to try our luck against them, even if it seemed a hopeless enterprise. . . Actually Mexico was a good deal stronger than he said, for it is one thing to have seen the place and its tremendous strength and quite another to describe it as I have."

Imagine wearing this while clanking along on a horse in a hot climate. This is the armor of a Spanish horse soldier, as displayed in the National Museum of History, Mexico City. It's not hard to see why some quickly adopted the wrapped fabric armor of Mexico's natives.

Then the great moment was at hand. They had crossed the last mountain barrier; now they gazed on the magnificence of the Valley of Mexico, the towns bordering the huge lake, the colorful temples wrapped in mist, the causeway leading straight to dazzling Tenochtitlán itself.

First they met a nephew of Moctezuma named Cacamatzin, who was carried on a litter richly decorated with green feathers, silver, gold and precious stones. Through Doña Marina, Cacamatzin said to Cortés. "We have come here, Malinche, to place ourselves at your disposal and to offer you whatever you want and to put you in our city, which is your home, for our great prince, Moctezuma, has ordered it so. He asks to be pardoned that he did not come to greet you himself but he is absent not because he bears ill will toward you but because of poor health."

And on the next day they marched along the causeway to the great city itself, meeting many curious citizens and more *caciques* (chieftains) along the way. Running through the mind of Diáz in those moments --- and surely through the minds of Cortés and the others --- were all the warnings they had received: BEWARE OF ENTERING THE CITY OF MEXICO BE—CAUSE ONCE YOU ARE INSIDE, THERE IS NO ESCAPE. YOU WILL ALL BE KILLED.

But they continued to advance. . .

Diáz wrote: "What men in the world have ever shown such daring?"

At last they were met by the great Moctezuma himself, accompanied by a large party of lords and *caciques*. When the Aztec ruler was helped from his litter, Diáz noted that his sandals had soles of gold. Held over him was a canopy of gold and silver embroidery. As Moctezuma slowly walked toward Cortés, his arms were held by chieftains while servants scurried ahead with brooms, sweeping the ground which his golden soles would touch.

Cortés dismounted and approached. Through Doña Marina, Moctezuma said, "I bid you welcome, Malinche."

Cortés wished the emperor good health, then told him that his heart rejoiced at having seen such a great prince. Then, following the emperor, Cortés and his company passed through huge crowds of curious citizens and entered the heart of the Aztec capital. Moctezuma ordered that they be given apartments in which to rest.

The date was November 8, 1519. It had been a strange episode, peaceful and polite. It couldn't last; neither the Spaniards nor the Aztecs were peaceful peoples.

OUTRAGE AT VILLA RICA

The two leaders fenced delicately during the first few days. They talked politely about many things. But tension grew steadily among the Spaniards as rumors rippled through their ranks. Soldiers began to mutter about stealing what gold they could carry, then getting off this tight little island which was beginning to feel like a prison . . . or a tomb.

Their fears were realized when Tlaxcalan messengers brought grim news: Villa Rica, the town established by the Spanish at the coast, had been attacked by Moctezuma's warriors and was in great danger of being wiped out!

On the very next day, Cortés and his men seized Moctezuma and imprisoned the great ruler in the Spanish quarters. Then Cortés ordered Moctezuma to send for the Mexican leaders who had committed the outrage against Villa Rica. When they appeared at Tenochtitlán, a sorrowing Moctezuma offered them to Cortés for punishment.

Cortés promptly ordered them burned in front of Moctezuma's palace. Yes, burned. Thinking that Moctezuma might interfere, Cortés had him chained, which enraged the emperor. But, according to Díaz, the terrible vengeance of Cortés had made Moctezuma even more afraid.

For the moment, Cortés was master of the situation. But only for the moment. Word arrived from the coast that a Spanish army of 900 men had landed, sent by Governor Velásquez of Cuba to whip Cortés! Velásquez was an old rival of Cortés; now he saw a chance to stab Cortés in the back.

Wondering how many enemies one man could fight at one time, Cortés had to leave Moctezuma in the charge of Pedro de Alvarado, a trusted lieutenant, then dash to the coast with most of his army. He met the Velásquez army in battle and won a great victory. Narváez, leader of the Velásquez expedition, was imprisoned.

When Cortés told the Narváez soldiers of the riches of Tenochtitlán, they reacted like Spaniards. They volunteered to join him on the return march. So now Cortés commanded a trained army of more than 1300 soldiers, 96 horses, 80 crossbowmen and as many musketeers, three times the strength with which he had first entered Tenochtitlán!

He would need them all. . . and more.

TROUBLE AT TENOCHTITLAN

The Narváez problem had barely been whipped when Tlaxcalans brought Cortés more shattering news: revolt had broken out in Tenochtitlán! The Spanish quarters had been attacked and set afire; seven soldiers had been killed and many others wounded.

There was nothing to do but start immediately for the capital. At this tense moment, messengers arrived from Moctezuma with a frightening confirmation of the story. Alvarado had given the Aztecs permission to celebrate a feast, then had attacked them, killing and wounding many. Tearfully, the messengers insisted that the Aztecs had been given no choice but to defend themselves.

Cortés sent an angry reply to Moctezuma, then quickly dispatched another message to Alvarado. He advised Alvarado that help was on the way and warned him that Moctezuma should be guarded carefully.

It was in late June, 1520, when Cortés and his reinforced army again clattered across the causeway into Tenochtitlán. This time there were no friendly Indians in the streets to greet them.

Except one --- Moctezuma, who appeared in the courtyard to welcome the Spanish leader. Cortés greeted him coldly. *El Capitán* plainly believed that Moctezuma had acted treacherously.

He was no more pleased with the officer he had left in charge. Alvarado admitted attacking the Indians, but said he had done it only because of rumors that the Aztecs planned to assault the Spanish as soon as the celebration ended.

Furious, Cortés told Alvarado what he thought of his bungling but there was no time for further argument.

A Spanish soldier, wounded and frantic, plunged into the quarters to report breathlessly that he had been attacked along his route from Tacuba, a nearby town. The road by which he had come and the city itself, he gasped, were filled with battle-ready warriors!

Immediately Cortés ordered Diego de Ordaz to lead 400 soldiers into the threatening streets.

They were stopped cold. Step by step, assaulted from all sides, the soldiers were forced to retreat toward the Spanish quarters. Then squadrons of screaming warriors attacked the quarters; a fierce battle raged for the rest of the day and throughout the night.

Díaz described the scene: "Still many Indians continued to assault us and they told us we were women and called us abusive names. . . for their daring was such that some attacked on one side and some on the other and they entered our quarters and set them afire. We could not endure the smoke and fire until we could throw earth over it and cut off other rooms from which fire came. In truth, they believed they could burn us alive. So many of them fell on us, and threw javelins and stones and arrows so that it looked like chaff on a threshing floor . . .

"Then when we would go out to burn their houses, they would raise the wooden drawbridges between the houses so that we could pass only through deep water. Then we could not bear rocks and stones hurled from roofs in such a way that many of us were wounded. Some three or four soldiers who had served in Italy swore to God that they had never seen such fierce fighting, not even when they had been in the battle between Christians and against the artillery of the King of France, or of the Great Turk, nor had they seen men like those Indians with such courage in closing up their ranks. . .

"Many other squadrons tried to enter our rooms and neither with guns, crossbows nor muskets, nor with many charges and sword thrusts could we force them back, for they cried out that not one of us should remain alive and they would sacrifice our hearts and blood to their gods, and there would be enough to glut their appetites and hold feasts on our arms and legs and would throw our bodies to the tigers, lions, vipers and snakes which they kept caged so that they might gorge on them, and for that reason they had not fed them for two days. As for the Tlaxcalans who were with us, they said they would place them in cages for fattening and would offer their bodies in sacrifice. Night after night, without end, there were screams and whistles and showers of stones, darts and arrows . . . "

In desperation the Spanish built what Díaz called "machines" --- wooden towers which would shield 25 soldiers as they edged out into the deadly streets. Using the towers as long as they held together, the Spaniards assaulted a well-defended pyramid near their quarters, fought their way up step by step and burned the idols at the top. It was a great victory but it was not enough to turn the tide.

Now Cortés saw that he must seek peace, at least for long enough to let them get out of this fearsome city. He could see only one way to bring this about: take Moctezuma onto the roof to talk to his angry, swarming people.

It was done. Moctezuma spoke but the soldiers who were supposed to protect him failed in their duty. Stones hurled from below struck Moctezuma in the head, arm and leg.

Díaz said that Moctezuma refused treatment. At any rate, the Aztec ruler soon died. He was carried out of the Spanish quarters by six captive Aztecs who told Cuitlahuac, the new emperor, how Moctezuma had been killed by his own people. (This is the Díaz version of Moctezuma's death, remember. Indian writers claimed that the emperor's body bore knife wounds, proving that the Spanish murdered him. The Díaz version makes more sense. By killing Moctezuma, the Spanish could only have made their desperate situation worse. Whatever Cortés may have been, he wasn't a fool.)

Grief-stricken, the Aztecs refused to talk of peace and attacked with even greater fury. Díaz said: "In fact we were staring death in the face. . . "

And so the decision was made to leave Tenochtitlán, thus setting the stage for a great, bloody climax of Mexican history: *La Noche Triste*, The Sad Night.

A NIGHT FOR DYING

For the desperate Spaniards, *La Noche Triste* began near midnight. The weather suited their situation: grim, dark and wet. The gaps in the causeway had been opened, so how could they escape?

Cortés had the answer: a portable wooden bridge had been built. It would be carried, put in place and guarded by 400 Tlaxcalans and 150 Spanish soldiers. When horses, personnel and baggage had crossed, the bridge would be moved to the next opening.

Baggage? Of course; no one would expect Spaniards to leave empty-handed. They were never so desperate that they would leave the loot behind. (Díaz said that the former soldiers of Narváez were especially greedy in packing up gold and other goodies; many would drown under the weight of their greed. Even Díaz, though, admitted to slipping a few jewels under his armor.)

In the dark of night, they began their departure, leaving only their dead. As they moved tensely toward the first opening in the causeway, there was no response. But they knew the city was filled with silent enemies, waiting . . .

The portable bridge was put in place and Cortés led the first detachment over it. Immediately thereafter, the Aztec version of hell broke loose.

From the roofs and from the streets, shouts and trumpet blasts and whistle shrieks tore the night apart. A message went out to thousands of canoes gliding through the dark on the lake, "Come out at once with your canoes and cut them off so that not one of them shall be left alive!"

Attacks exploded from all directions, from the lake, from the roofs, from both sides of the bridge. Indians assaulted the bridge so fiercely that it could not be moved. The opening quickly filled up with screaming horses, human bodies and rich baggage. On the far side of the bridge, Cortés and his soldiers sent their horses charging into the wall of lances facing them and broke through, only to find themselves under attack on one side of the causeway from roofs, on the other from warriors in canoes. The muskets and the crossbows had been lost at the bridge, so in this terrible moment the Spanish could do little but run.

This stump in Mexico City may have a history. This, they say, is what remains of the tree under which Hernán Cortés rested after being thrown out of Tenochtitlán. It's called "El Arbol de la Noche Triste" and we all want to believe it's the real thing, which is why the stump has a fence around it.

Planned retreat became panicky flight. Cortés, finally safe on the mainland, heard of the disaster at the bridge. He immediately spurred back onto the causeway, only to meet Pedro de Alvarado, wounded and afoot, with four Spaniards and eight Tlaxcalans all wounded many times.

They had escaped, reported Alvarado, only by struggling across the mass of bodies at the bridge. Alvarado himself had been forced to plunge his lance into the lake bed, then vault across the opening, armor and all! The enemy now swarmed over all the causeways; there would be no more survivors.

There was nothing for Cortés to do then but return in sadness to the mainland.

But *La Noche Triste* had only begun. Licking their wounds, the torn-up remnants of Cortés's once-proud army gathered at dawn near a large cypress tree, then moved north in an attempt to escape the relentless Indian forces which still attacked them and drew even more blood.

Once around the great lake, they could turn toward Tlaxcala and safety. But many more would die before Tlaxcala. . .

Taking stock in Tlaxcala, Díaz sadly counted a mere 440 soldiers left out of more than 1300 Spaniards who had marched into Tenochtitlán. All of the survivors were wounded.

Any lesser man in charge of such a group would have headed back to Cuba with his tail between his legs. Not Hernán Cortés.

Only 22 days after crawling into Tlaxcala, beaten and bloody, Cortés ordered his company out for an attack on a nearby village! Only a few months later, this incredible leader had put together a force of 600 well-armed Spaniards, 40 horses, 13 ships and the best of Tlaxcala's warriors and was ready to march again on Tenochtitlán!

Thirteen ships? Exactly. This time the Spanish brought a navy. Remembering those thousands of canoes in the lake on *La Noche Triste*, Cortés had collected the hardware from the burned ships at the coast and put his marine carpenters to work cutting timbers. Then he enlisted 6000 Tlaxcalans to carry the materials to Texcoco, on the shore of the great lake. From this material would be built 13 small sailing vessels called brigantines.

With cannon and soldiers aboard, it was expected that they would cut a wide gap through the swarming canoes of the Aztecs.

FIGHT TO A FINISH

In midwinter of the year 1520, the Aztec empire was not in the best of shape for self defense.

Moctezuma's successor, Cuitlahuac, had died of smallpox, which had been introduced at Veracruz the year before. Infected Indians had perished by the thousands.

The new emperor was a very young nephew of Moctezuma named Cuauhtémoc, who vowed that Tenochtitlán would be defended as long as a single Aztec remained alive. It was not an idle boast.

But Cuauhtémoc was facing a military genius in Hernán Cortés. Now this genius had gained the support of most of the Indians outside of Tenochtitlán. These Indians knew very well that now it was not the Spanish who were trapped in Tenochtitlán but the Aztecs themselves.

Cortés cut off the conduits which brought fresh water into the city along the causeways. He laid waste the lakeshore so that night-foraging parties of food hunters had to return to the island empty-handed and hungry.

This is not to say it was easy for Cortés, even with all his advantages. He had to assault the city for 93 days, marching over the causeways to fight in the morning, then returning to the safe mainland to sleep, day after bloody day. Yet Cuauhtémoc would not surrender . . .

Cortés and company went into the town daily and burned houses, first along the causeways, then in the city itself. They threatened to burn the city to the ground and tear down temples and pyramids. Yet Cuauhtémoc would not surrender . . .

The Spanish brigantines, in what must be one of the strangest naval battles of all time, sailed boldly into the lake to run down the canoes. Then they chased survivors into the canals of the city itself. It was reported to the Spanish that old women appeared in the vacant streets of the city at night, looking for scraps of anything to eat. Yet Cuauhtémoc would not surrender . . .

This is downtown Tenochtitlán. Models of the Aztec capital may be seen at several museums in Mexico City. Note temples atop pyramids. It's not hard to understand why the Spaniards were dazzled.

In their daily commute to the city for battle, the Spaniards suffered, too. On one night remembered all too clearly by Díaz, they had retired to their camp on the causeway but could not rest; drums and trumpets assaulted their ears and drew their eyes toward a great pyramid in the center of Tenochtitlán.

" . . . and saw that our comrades whom they had captured were being carried by force up the steps and were going to be sacrificed. When they got them up to a small square in front of the temple where their terrible idols are kept, they put plumes on their heads and with fans in their hands forced them to dance before Huitzilopochtli and after they danced they were placed on their backs and with stone knives their hearts were cut out and the skin was flayed off their faces . . . It should also be noted that we were not far away from them, yet we could give them no help and we could only pray to God to keep us from such a death."

Díaz also spoke of a "cursed drum" which sounded from the top of a pyramid on the nights of sacrifices. Combined with whistling and yelling and great bonfires, the result was a hair-raising sound-and-light show which grated hard on Spanish nerves.

We would call it "psychological warfare." Against a weaker foe, it might have worked. But this time the odds against the Aztecs were too great.

END OF AN EMPIRE

Dried-out and starving, the Aztecs were driven into one small quarter of their once proud city. Yet Cuauhtémoc refused to surrender . . .

Cortés threatened to level the city, building by building. He got well started on the job, too, but the Aztecs continued to fight. On the last day of battle, according to Díaz, dead and prisoners exceeded 12,000 persons. When the Spanish finally approached the city's last fort, they had to climb over the dead piled high in the streets!

Cuauhtémoc was captured and brought before Cortés.

"Señor Malinche," Díaz quotes Cuauhtémoc, "I have surely done my duty in defending my city and I can do no more. I come into your presence as a prisoner. Take the dagger you have in your belt and kill me at once."

Cortés refused. Instead he expressed admiration for the Indian leader, went with him and his family to Coyoacán on the mainland. The date: August 13, 1521. Darkness was gathering as they passed through the bleeding carcass of the once majestic city. It began to rain and the rain washed blood into the canals.

At the time of his capture, Cuauhtémoc, according to both Díaz and Cortés, was only 18 years old! He was not fated to get much older.

Cortés expressed great friendship for the defeated leader but allowed him to be tortured. Cuauhtémoc refused to tell the hiding place of Aztec treasure, saying it had all been stolen.

Hot oil was applied to his feet again and again, burning and crippling him, but the incredible Cuauhtémoc would say no more.

In 1524, Cortés marched toward Central America to straighten out a Spanish colonization effort there. Not daring to leave Cuauhtémoc and other chieftains in Mexico City, he took them along. During the course of a difficult journey, rumors arose of revolt brewing among the Indians. By order of Cortés, Cuauhtémoc was hanged.

After having been given up for lost, Cortés returned to the capital to find that his power had melted away. He had been greeted as a saviour in many villages along his return route. The villagers had suffered terribly under the Spanish vultures who had ruled in the absence of Cortés. And in the capital, the now powerful vultures continued to peck at Cortés.

In 1527, Cortés sailed to Spain in a desperate attempt to make his case before King Charles V. Charles was polite, no more. Cortés was given huge tracts of land in southern Mexico and a resounding title; however, his power was not restored. Nuño de Guzmán, an inhuman monster, had grabbed the hangman's rope and was not about to let go.

Pushed into the background, slipping into middle age, Hernán Cortés had to spend his time developing his *ranchos*. He

The palace of Cortés in Cuernavaca is now restored and used as a museum.

introduced much that was new to Mexican agriculture. He planted mulberry trees and started silk culture; he brought cattle and sheep and mules into the country; he planted fruit trees, wheat and sugar cane and established the first sugar mills. He also worked mightily to establish the Catholic church in Mexico. In fact, the wealth and influence of Cortés again grew to a point where he attracted the attention of the vultures in the capital.

In one final attempt to regain the favor of his king, Cortés sailed to Spain in 1539. He failed. He was a giant among gnats but enough gnats can bring down any giant.

Bitter and neglected, Cortés died in Spain in 1547. He had asked that his body be returned to his beloved Mexico; it was done. His remains first were buried in a convent in Texcoco, on the shore of the lake which had seen his greatest triumph. More than 200 years later, the bones of Cortés were moved to his favorite charity, Hospital Jesús de Nazareno in Mexico City.

But still the vultures pecked at him. During the war for independence from Spain, feeling ran so high against the Spanish that a few supporters of Cortés found it necessary to hide the casket in a wall of the hospital. The casket was not discovered until 1946.

The greatest of all *conquistadores*, restless in death as in life, is entombed in the hospital today.

You will find no statues of Cortés in Mexico, nor streets bearing his name; only his palace in Cuernavaca has been restored as a museum. The name of the young man defeated by Cortés, Cuauhtémoc, is honored throughout the land; his statue tops an impressive column along Mexico City's most important avenue.

Yet Cortés, roaring *"Santiago!"* as he spurred his horse in charge after daring charge could not have conquered without the help of the Tlaxcalans and Cempoalans and other Indians --- natives of Mexico. To them, he was a saviour.

Cruel conqueror? Or saviour? Some day Mexicans may be willing to see Hernán Cortés as both.

THREE
--- The Colonial Years

MOCTEZUMA'S REVENGE

There is an old saying: "To the victor belongs the spoils."

There should be another old saying: "Sometimes spoils stick in your throat."

In New Spain after the crushing of the Aztecs, the *conquistadores* were disappointed at first. Instead of piles of gold, they found slim pickings. But the wealth was there in fantastic amounts, right under their dusty boots.

Food from the land and silver from under the land would make Spain rich. Then the same riches would turn Spain into a starving beggar. Moctezuma, had he lived to see it, might have smiled and murmured a few words about the rewards of greed.

Spain ruled Mexico for about 300 years. In 1535, only a few years after the conquest, Mexico City had its first mint in

Typical working conditions in an old-style Mexican mine. Note ladder in background, with peons climbing.

operation. Soon thereafter a small stream of silver coins from the mint trickled into Europe. Then, in 1547, some Spanish soldiers were camping in the Guanajuato area. After starting a warming fire on a rock, they were startled by the sight of shiny puddles beneath the flames. Silver! The area was loaded with the precious stuff. In 1557, a new process for separating silver from its ore was discovered. With this, Mexico was on its way to flooding the world with its riches.

Shiny Spanish dollars, stamped out by wooden machines, flowed out of the Mexico City mint, Casa de Moneda. This mint and others eventually would produce about two billion dollars worth of coin, most of which was shipped to a Europe still counting pennies. Silver bars exported amounted to a couple of billion more.

Before the rich flood petered out, there had been shipped through the Mexican port of Veracruz two-thirds of the total silver supply of the world at that time! A single mine in Zacatecas is said to have produced 20 per cent of the world's silver before 1800!

So Spain got rich quick, right? Well, a few Spaniards got rich. The rest starved. Spain was a monarchy, remember. Most of the incoming riches were skimmed by the king and his cronies to finance all sorts of grand schemes, like wars against irritating neighbors.

The little which trickled down wasn't enough to sustain life for the average Spaniard. The common man's curse was something called "inflation." Sound familiar? The wealth of New Spain brought the world's first serious inflation to Old Spain, wiping out its economy, its government and its way of life. Spain still struggles today to escape from that economic quicksand.

When the silver flow slowed, Spain's rulers had gotten used to living high. Taxes were raised to offset the dropping income from the mines of Mexico. Loans were arranged, then more loans, until generations yet unborn had been committed to pay Spanish debts. Government positions were sold to raise money for the crown; titles of nobility were auctioned off; soldiers went

unpaid and rioted in foreign lands. Eventually Spain went bankrupt under Phillip II and took down with it great banks in Germany and Italy.

Mexican silver had done it, first by flowing in what seemed
to be an endless river, then by drying up.

Moctezuma's revenge . . .

TEMPLES COME TUMBLING DOWN

The shining island city of Tenochtitlán was about to disappear into the mists of memory. Wounded terribly during the
war, the city had only begun to suffer.

Soon after the conquest, Hernán Cortés wiped it out, destroyed it, erased it from the face of the earth. Why? There is
evidence that Cortés wanted no trace of Aztec power to remain.
So, stone by stone, the temples and palaces and houses came
down and were dumped into the canals.

But now there was a need for a new capital, a heart of government which would pump blood through the arteries of New
Spain. But where to build it?

Cortés chose the island. It had been the seat of the old
empire; now it would be the seat of the new. So tens of thousands of Indians were put to work building a Spanish city. In
1524, Cortés was able to write his emperor:

"They have accomplished much and now the city is populated with 30,000 families and is just as orderly as before. Also,
I have granted them such liberties and immunities that they will
increase greatly. They live very much as they please and many
artisans make a living among us, such as carpenters, masons,
stonecutters and silversmiths . . . Merchants do business in safety; others fish for a living and others farm and there are already
many who have plantations sown with all manner of vegetables
that we have received from Spain. I assure Your Majesty that if
we could obtain more plants and seeds from Spain, the ability
of these natives in cultivating the earth and establishing plantations is such that they would shortly produce an abundance and
great profit would come to the imperial crown. I beg Your Majesty to order that no ship be allowed to sail without bringing a
certain number of plants . . . "

The old shrine of Guadalupe and the chapel next door are sinking into the old lake bed. This photo, taken before the painting of the Virgin was moved, shows believers on their knees making their painful pilgrimage. The Hill of Tepeyac, where Juan Diego saw his vision, is in background.

How times had changed! Not too many years earlier, Cortés had cried out for soldiers, horses and arms. Cortés the Conqueror was becoming Cortés the Builder.

Small men make small mistakes. Great men, like Cortés, have it within them to make enormous mistakes. When Cortés decided to build the capital of New Spain on an island in the lake, he wanted to make it a monument. What he made was a disaster.

The reason is simple: the great Valley of Mexico is an enormous water trap. The lake in which Tenochtitlán was built had no outlets. During the rainy season (which is summer in most of Mexico), water sluiced down the slopes of the great mountains surrounding the valley, then sloshed across the valley floor into an enormous lake. Evaporation of water under the eternal Mexican sun kept things in balance, more or less. In wet years, the Aztec homes had swimming pools nearby; in dry years, the lake shrank and dead fish perfumed the evening air.

As the city grew, the lake got in the way. Not many people want to live on houseboats or plant gardens on *chinampas,* so the solution was to empty the lake by cutting a ditch through a canyon leading out of the valley.

Presto! Dry land . . . sort of. In fact, it was mostly silt washed down from the mountains with the rains of centuries. As a result, many of Mexico City's oldest and most important buildings today tilt crazily. City officials wonder if their metropolis will sink out of sight, wash away in a wet year or smother in the throat-charring smog which now fills the ancient valley of the Aztecs.

A new building, firmly set on pilings buried in the lake bed, seems to rise, year by year, but it isn't really rising; the old building next to it, unsupported by pilings, is simply sinking. The Palace of Fine Arts, a city showplace, has dropped four meters; what was once its ground floor is now its basement. The old Basilica de Guadalupe, much-loved mother church of Mexico's peasants, tilts alarmingly and threatens to topple onto the chapel next door. Or is it the chapel which leans in the other direction? In Mexico City, one never knows.

As has been mentioned, Mexicans, by and large, are not admirers of Hernán Cortés. It they could send a message to his bones in Hospital de Jesús in the sagging center of Mexico City, it might go something like this: "Señor, you built this city in the wrong place. God willing, may you sink into the mud with the rest of us."

It could happen.

It is worth repeating that there were two kinds of wealth in New Spain: precious minerals and cropland. But perhaps it was the Indian population which made up the real wealth of the country, as far as the Spanish were concerned. The typical Spaniard in New Spain sneered at manual labor; after all, he hadn't crossed the ocean to grub in the dirt. But somebody had to work the mines and farms and pack supplies or the whole grand scheme would fall on its face.

The Spanish had a system and it worked for a time. Called *encomienda*, it had been used in Spain to govern Moorish provinces. Put simply, it was legal slavery. If the Spanish crown could give land grants to its favored sons, why couldn't it also hand over people to work the land? The people, of course, were Indians. The Spanish slavemaster was called *encomendero*.

And what kind of work did the Indians do? Much of it was unbelievably hard. In one of the richest mines, Valenciana at Guanajuato, ore had to be carried 457 meters to the surface. Hoisting machinery wasn't used until late in the 18th century. The work was done by Indian laborers breathing bad air at lower levels, climbing 457-meter ladders with 45-kilo sacks of ore on their backs!

The Spanish introduced pack animals to Mexico but there were never enough to go around. Also, the terrain was even too difficult for mules at times. It was lucky for the Spanish that Mexicans had developed a professional class of porters called *tamemes*, who could carry huge loads for great distances. (Remember those Tlaxcalans who carried Cortés's ships to Lake Texcoco?)

Spanish Bishop Juan de Zumárraga wrote in an angry letter in 1529:

An old system still in use in many parts of Mexico is this irrigation wheel photographed near San Luis Potosí. They might be powered by foot, as this one is, or by hand or by mule.

"The Indians are much abused by Spanish travelers, who load them like pack animals and take them wherever they wish to go . . . the Indians suffer great harm and even die along the road. It is worst among the gold miners, who load the Indians of their *encomiendas* heavily and send them as far as 50 leagues and many die along the way. I know of one province called Tepeaca from which it is said that more than 3000 free men. . . have died on the road from carrying supplies to the mines."

In places, it was said, the bleaching bones of *tamemes* lay in piles along the trails.

It is estimated that the central plateau of Mexico, the most heavily populated region then and now, could count at least 11 million persons in 1521, at the time of the Spanish conquest. It is also estimated that by 1600, the population had dropped by 90 per cent. Ninety per cent!

Never say to an Indian *tameme*, "Hard work never hurt anybody."

But, of course, more than overwork was involved. The Spanish introduced smallpox; there were terrible epidemics in 1520, 1531 and 1545. Typhoid fever, measles, malaria and yellow fever also took a grim toll.

GOOD MEN AND BAD

Beltrán Nuño de Guzmán . . . it doesn't seem possible that anyone could come down through history with the rotten reputation this man bears. But it must be remembered: Nuño de Guzmán worked at it.

Cortés and other *conquistadores* were useful to the crown (and to the Council of the Indies, which actually ran the show in New Spain) as long as they were doing their thing, which was mostly physical combat. But once the blood was washed away, *conquistadores* were war surplus, like their armor and cannons.

Feeling like war surplus, Cortés sailed from Veracruz for Spain in 1527. Meanwhile, the crown set up the first *Audencia* of Mexico. An *Audencia* was a kind of supreme court, city council and legislature, mixed into one official pie. President of the *Audencia*: Beltrán Nuño de Guzmán.

His main qualification for the job seems to have been his hatred for Cortés, or perhaps, for the human race. As governor

A Mexican tameme, this one only 12 years old! His load weighs about 34 kilograms (about 75 pounds).

of the province of Panuco, he captured and sent into slavery 21 shiploads of human beings. He almost completely depopulated several provinces of Mexico with his slave raids and his career was then only beginning.

Two years after Nuño de Guzmán had been installed as *Audencia* president, his murders began to haunt him. His particular enemy was Bishop Zumárraga, a friend of Cortés, who had been trying for some time to sneak a report on Nuño de Guzmán's devilment back to Spain. But the president censored all messages passing through Veracruz, so the bishop had to go there himself. In the seaport, he located a sailor from his home province in Spain and arranged a bit of smuggling. The bishop's letter was hidden in a cake of wax, then popped into a barrel of oil.

Delivered to the Council of the Indies, the letter was a blockbuster. New Spain was raised to the status of viceroyalty and the new viceroy would outrank Nuño de Guzmán. Now the crown would have better control of Mexico.

Nuño de Guzmán decided that the climate of the capital no longer suited him, so he put together an army of troublemakers. Then he blazed a bloody trail through the western provinces, which he named New Galicia. Along the way he enjoyed his hobbies of burning, hanging and enslaving. He was allowed to run wild for seven more years but finally was shipped back to Spain in disgrace. Considering his crimes, it was a slap on the wrist.

One thing can be said for Nuño de Guzmán: he made almost everyone who followed him in New Spain look good by comparison.

A great fiesta lit up Mexico City in November, 1535. There were games and music, parades and free food for everyone. The occasion was the arrival of Don Antonio de Mendoza, a member of one of the great families of Spain. He bore the heavy title: Viceroy, Governor-General and President of the *Audencia* of New Spain.

No longer would the riches and the people of New Spain be at the mercy of creatures like Nuño de Guzmán. Mendoza added a strong touch of class; heads lifted in pride again.

73

Except one head, that of Hernán Cortés, who had hoped to be appointed viceroy. It was not to be. Don Antonio de Mendoza was at least as clever as the great *conquistador* and was backed by the crown, besides.

Conquistadores had conquered Mexico; now Don Antonio, agent of the crown, had to snatch Mexico back from the *conquistadores*. Meaning, mainly, Hernán Cortés. In his spare time, the viceroy had only to construct roads and towns, administer law throughout the country, protect the crown income, establish and maintain all sorts of public services, develop farming, mining and commerce. Then, during his coffee breaks, Don Antonio could always work on the Indian problem. Prodded by priests, he struggled to save the Indians from exploitation or worse.

And then there was the tourist business . . .

THE RICH TRY TO GET RICHER

A certain Alvar Núñez Cabeza de Vaca had first told of the marvelous cities. He had spent eight years in wandering over a vast area consisting of today's southern U.S. and northern Mexico. Feverish rumors swept New Spain. Just how rich were the "Seven Cities of Cibola"?

Viceroy Mendoza quickly sent a trusted agent, Fray Marcos, to investigate.

"Larger than the city of Mexico," sang the excited priest on his return, describing a metropolis he had seen in the distance. Even before Fray Marcos had come back with stirring news, Viceroy Mendoza had dug deep into his treasury to equip a large expedition under Francisco Vásquez de Coronado.

The expedition was a wild goose chase which cost many lives and much money. Stories of the Seven Cities had apparently been triggered by sightings of the Indian pueblos of New Mexico. Fray Marcos supposedly carved his name on a rock near Santa Fe, New Mexico.

The Spanish crown was furious about the Coronado expedition; Mendoza was ordered to stop chasing ghosts. One reason the crown was so unhappy was that the Coronado expedition, by draining off soldiers from New Galicia, made possible the so-called Mixtón War, the only serious Indian uprising

This sample cutaway of a Zapotec thatched hut is in the Museum of Anthropology, Mexico City.

during the three centuries of Spanish rule. Semi-barbaric Indians, called *Chichemecas* or "wild men" by Mexicans, chose this moment of Spanish weakness to avenge the wrongs they had suffered under Nuño de Guzmán's reign of terror. The revolt was put down but not before *Conquistador* Pedro de Alvarado was beaten in battle with the Indians, then killed by a falling horse. It was a dismal end for this battle-scarred veteran of the Tenochtitlán causeways.

Mendoza probably was able to control his grief; now he had one less *conquistador* to worry about. Also, Mendoza inherited Alvarado's fleet of ships, anchored in Pacific ports.

Ships? Small, cobbled-up tubs is what they really were. But, with the right captains and crews, they would make maritime history.

If the land explorations were sometimes embarrassing, the sea adventures were often glorious. Especially successful were the voyages of Ruy López de Villalobos to the East Indies and Juan Rodríguez Cabrillo along the coast of California.

SIXTY-ONE VICEROYS, ALL IN A ROW

Most of the viceroys who governed Mexico were not as good as Mendoza, nor as bad as Nuño de Guzmán. The portraits of all 61 of them hang in Chapultepec Castle, Mexico City, now a national history museum. Some of the viceroys were strong and wise, some were cruel, some were stupid, some were no more than bookkeepers for the crown. Each, though, left his stamp on modern Mexico.

Spanish rule in Mexico failed not because the viceroys failed but because Spain wore itself out in a series of silly wars in Europe. The riches of Mexico lured the rulers of Spain into making some stupid mistakes. Then the royal house came tumbling down and Mexico tumbled with it.

They call it "Plaza of the Three Cultures"; it is in Mexico City's Tlatelolco district. (Tlatelolco once was the major suburb of Tenochtitlán.) The centerpiece of the plaza is a partial reconstruction of an Aztec pyramid and ball court. Nearby is a famous church of the Spanish period. Surrounding the area are high-rise modern buildings, offices and apartments. Three cultures --- old, not-so-old and new.

A marble plaque in front of the church announces:

"THE THIRTEENTH OF AUGUST OF 1521, HEROI-CALLY DEFENDED BY CUAUHTEMOC, TLATELOLCO FELL UNDER THE POWER OF HERNAN CORTES. IT WAS NOT A TRIUMPH NOR A DEFEAT, IT WAS THE PAINFUL BIRTH OF THE MIXED RACE THAT IS THE MEXICO OF TODAY."

And so it was. As the 19th century began, Mexico had three kinds of people: *gachupines*, the rich ruling class, born in Spain; *criollos* (creoles), of Spanish blood but born in Mexico; *mestizos*, the mixed race of Indians and Spaniards and blacks. Plus a few pure Indians on the fringes, pitifully few.

Gachupines were top dogs and they let the *criollos* and *mestizos* know it. *Criollos* were the middle class and were constantly squeezed from both ends. *Mestizos* lived at the bottom of the pile, ready for any change because it had to be an improvement. *Mestizos* and *criollos* were united in one thing only: hatred of *gachupines*.

There had been many *tumultos* (riots) led by *criollos*. All had been crushed by the *gachupines*. But the pressure continued to build. The final explosion was triggered not in Mexico but in Europe. by the kidnapping of a king.

Napoleon of France recklessly snatched King Charles IV and Crown Prince Ferdinand of Spain in 1808; then Napoleon put Joseph Bonaparte on the throne of Spain. It was as if Mexico had suddenly been cut adrift from the mother country. Both *criollos* and *gachupines* grabbed eagerly at the loose reins of power.

In the dark of night on September 15, 1808, the *gachupines* won the first round by attacking the palace in Mexico City, arresting the viceroy and replacing him with a doddering old man named Garibay. The *criollos* went underground, grumbling and plotting.

Among them was a *criollo* priest in the village of Dolores in the state of Guanajuato. The match he struck on the steps of his country church touched off revolutionary flames which would sweep like hellfire over the length and breadth of Mexico.

Suddenly the war cry echoed off the mountains and rattled through the valleys:

"DEATH TO *GACHUPINES!* DEATH!"

FOUR
--- The Breakaway

VIVA INDEPENDENCIA!
VIVA MEXICO!

It is a strange building, this "Alhóndiga." Tourists strolling down the long canyon which cradles the town of Guanajuato stare at it and wonder. Unless they know the story, of course.

At each of the building's four corners, high, a name is engraved in the masonry. Once there were cages hanging from hooks at each corner. In each cage was a decaying head --- a human head. In time, the cages held only skulls. The skulls remained until Mexico was at last free of Spanish rule.

They are Mexican heroes, all four. Three of the names at the corners are "Aldama," "Jiménez," and "Allende." The fourth is "Hidalgo."

Hidalgo . . .

A town is not a town in Mexico unless it has a street or a market or a school bearing his name. Statues, paintings, relics --- they are everywhere. Most sacred of the relics is a bell which hangs at the National Palace in Mexico City. The bell is over a balcony facing the great Zócalo. On the night of September 16 each year, the president of Mexico takes great pride and pleasure in ringing that bell. In the Zócalo, tens of thousands of Mexicans roar: *"Viva Independencia! Viva Mexico!"*

Alhóndiga in Guanajuato. Hidalgo's head hung in a cage at this corner. The doorway at right was set afire by Pípila.

The bell came from the little town of Dolores, in the state of Guanajuato. The ceremony is called *"El Grito de Dolores."* *El Grito* means "The Shout."

The Shout still echoes in Mexico and not only on Independence Day. What does it matter the ceremony in the capital on September 16 uses words that were not used in 1810? What does it matter that the man Hidalgo was not perfect?

Mexico without *El Grito de Dolores* would not be Mexico.

In a way, the whole thing was an accident. That is, it wasn't supposed to happen when it did. Nothing unusual there; history is often made by accident.

His name was Miguel Hidalgo. He became Father Miguel Hidalgo at age 26. As a priest, he first taught at the College of San Nicolas in Valladolid (now Morelia).

In history, Father Hidalgo is a strange case. He was a priest but he was not the purest one who ever lived; he had some bad personal habits. He became a military leader but he wasn't very good at it. He set off a revolution, but the revolution failed.

So why did such a loser become a legendary hero whose praises are sung over the length and breadth of Mexico?

Because the man had great courage, and Mexicans admire courage. Because the man was a friend of Mexico's Indians at a time when those Indians had few friends. Because the man gave his life for Mexico.

Hidalgo was a *criollo*. That is, of Spanish blood but born in Mexico. First as a young student, then later as a teacher, he spent much time studying Indian languages. Father Hidalgo did so well in his early career that he became rector (president) of the College of San Nicolas in 1790. He lasted only five years; then he was fired.

The problem was money. Very simply, he had a bad habit of spending more than he took in. He wasn't putting the money in his own pocket; he was using it to improve living conditions for the students at the college.

And this is the way it was to be for Father Hidalgo. He usually had good intentions, but he often couldn't quite carry them out.

This strong sculpture of Hidalgo is in a proper place, the museum in the Alhóndiga of Guanajuato.

HIDALGC

He wound up as a parish priest in the quiet little town of Dolores. The unimportant village was to be his springboard into history.

THE PARTYING PRIEST

It was a good life in Dolores, maybe too good. Father Hidalgo loved parties; his house was the scene of many lively ones. Hidalgo allowed his assistants to handle many of the routine duties of the parish. This left him much time to read and write and discuss current ideas with his friends. Some of those ideas had drifted in from France, which had recently suffered through a great revolution and now was trying to make a working government out of "Liberty, Equality and Fraternity," the revolutionary slogan.

Hidalgo may not have been much of a bookkeeper but he knew how to make a parish prosper. It was against the law to make wine, but Hidalgo encouraged winemaking in his parish. He developed other industries, too, like pottery, silk culture, weaving and carpentry. The mining center of Guanajuato was nearby, so there was a ready market for the products of Dolores.

It must have been a satisfying life for Hidalgo, now well into middle age. So why would he want to blow that life into little bits?

In the church as elsewhere, *gachupines* --- Spaniards born in Spain --- held most of the power and plucked most of the plums. *Criollos* were offered the leavings. Hidalgo, the *criollo*, might well have felt resentment.

Hidalgo had mingled with Indians for most of his life. He loved them and was loved in return. He had watched Indians being ground under Spanish heels for a long time.

The *gachupines*, remember, had made a move to tighten their grip in 1808. Outnumbered by *criollos*, they had good reason to worry. Then, too, with the Spanish crown under the thumb of France, *gachupines* could expect no help from the mother country in case of trouble. *Gachupines* knew that unless they held the reins of power tightly, a few wild horses could snatch them away.

Hidalgo's church in the town of Dolores Hidalgo is a good deal fancier now than it was in 1810. Many presidents of Mexico have come here to recite El Grito de Dolores. Naturally they would want a proper background for the patriotic ceremony. Hidalgo's home, now a museum, is nearby.

In the area around Guanajuato, in the towns of Dolores and San Miguel and Querétaro, the wild horses were gathering, snorting and pawing . . .

ALLENDE, THE SOLDIER

Captain Ignacio Allende, the cavalry officer stationed in San Miguel, liked parties, too, and had an eye for pretty ladies. He also had a restless spirit and hated *gachupines*. Given this much in common, Captain Allende and Father Hidalgo were certain to hear about each other and to get together across the few kilometers which separated their towns.

But Hidalgo and Allende, who marched together into history, were not peas in a pod. One, Hidalgo, was a thinker and speaker. The other was a man of action. Hidalgo could stir up the troops with a rousing sermon; Allende, the military expert, could lead them into battle. Hidalgo knew where they wanted to go; Allende knew how to get there.

To those who were in on the early plotting and planning, the priest and the soldier must have looked like a winning team.

But there were a few small cracks in the mirror. Hidalgo loved Indians; Allende thought of them as a faceless mob. Allende believed that battles were won by trained troops moving against the enemy in disciplined ranks.

Hidalgo believed that enough Indians, throwing enough stones, could whip any royalist army. And that he, Hidalgo, was the one to lead them . . .

The plotting soon became hot and heavy. Every town of any size sprouted a revolutionary unit. The big question arose: should Indians and *mestizos* be invited to the party? Or were there enough *criollos* to pull it off?

There were a million *criollos*; they outnumbered *gachupines* by 70 to one! The odds seemed safe enough. But not all *criollos* could be depended upon. Some of them, mainly the richer ones, thought of themselves as Europeans, not Mexicans. And the *gachupines*, it must be remembered, controlled many army units, especially in and around the capital.

Criollo plotters talked like this:

Who hates *gachupines* more than anybody? Indians, of course. So they aren't soldiers. So they can't shoot guns to kill

Hidalgo's revolution was an informal affair in more ways than one. Common costumes were those of the Indian peasant at left; the regular army officer, center; the cowboy-rancher at right.

gachupines. Ten thousand Indians screaming and yelling and throwing stones might scare some to death. The decision was made to include the Indians.

Once that decision was reached, the next one was easy. Father Hidalgo would lead the revolt. The Indians would follow him.

Very early on the morning of September 16, a horse and rider clattered through the dark streets of the sleeping town of Dolores. The hurrying rider was Juan de Aldama, who had ridden the 80 kilometers from Querétaro with shattering news for Father Hidalgo: some of their fellow plotters had been arrested in Querétaro and their arms had been destroyed!

In that tense moment, Hidalgo faced a hard choice. They had planned to kick off the revolt in early October. Should they give themselves up now and take their chances with the royalist courts? Or should they run and hide? Or, since most of their arms were ready and plans made, should they touch off the flame?

Father Hidalgo had plotted too long to give it all up.

One witness in Dolores on that fateful night has Hidalgo saying, "Gentlemen, we are lost, there is no recourse but to go and seize *gachupines.*"

Another has him saying, "In action everything is accomplished; we must not lose time. You will all see the oppressor's yoke broken and beaten into the ground."

This much at least is clear: Father Hidalgo made a short speech in Dolores shortly before dawn. Most accounts have him speaking to a group from the steps of his church. But one account has him speaking from a window of his house; still another from the entrance hall. Wherever he spoke, whatever he said, it was this speech of Hidalgo's which is now called *El Grito.* . . The Shout.

And so the cry of liberation went out from the town of Dolores at dawn. Fourteen pottery workers and 31 soldiers from a unit stationed in the town were assembled; this was hardly enough for a good brawl, much less a revolution. But luckily, September 16 was a Sunday. By 8 a.m., 800 persons had gathered for mass and market day.

By the end of that fateful day, Father Hidalgo had led his "army" to San Miguel, Captain Allende's native city. The royalists there put up little resistance. The first *gachupines* were captured and imprisoned. In the flush of victory, Father Hidalgo adopted the banner of the Virgin of Guadalupe as the symbol of the revolution.

But there was a bad sign, too. In San Miguel, with the revolt less than one day old, Hidalgo's Indians got out of control. Before an angry Captain Allende could stop the violence, some *gachupín* houses and stores had been wrecked.

The military man might well have said to Hidalgo, "See? I told you so."

Five days later, the town of Celaya surrendered to a growing army of revolutionists. Surrender came only after Hidalgo threatened to kill Spanish hostages taken by his men. On this same day, Allende and the priest tried to tighten up their army's organization. Plainly enjoying his role, Father Hidalgo gave himself a splendid title: "Captain General of the Americas."

Another bad sign . . .

Leaving Dolores on September 16, the rebel army had consisted of fewer than 1000 persons. Leaving Celaya on September 23, there were 25,000!

A secret agent reported to the crown that of these, 9000 were Indian foot soldiers armed only with bows and arrows, clubs and slings. Four thousand more carried lances and machetes. About 12,000 more were mounted but only 100 of these horsemen were trained soldiers.

It was not an army; it was a mob. They didn't march; they straggled. A royalist taken captive described their slow progress in this way: "The Indians walked carrying their children, sheep, quarters of beef, and in the way of plunder, they carry doors, chairs and even beams on their shoulders."

But even with such burdens, the insurgents were moving. Next target: Guanajuato, No. 2 city of the realm, home of many rich and powerful *gachupines.*

Now Hidalgo and Allende let themselves hope that their revolution might turn into a triumphal march on the capital.

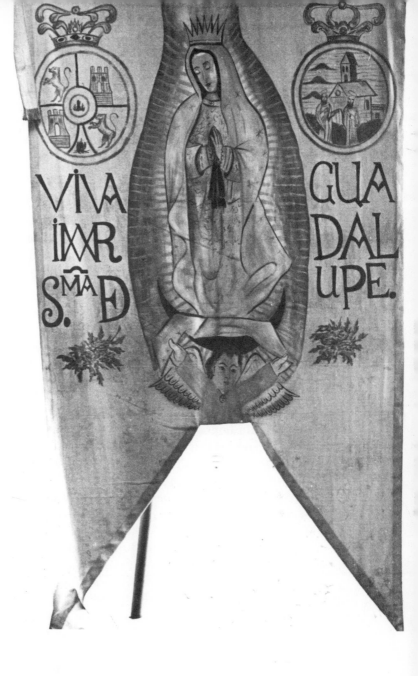

The banner of the Virgin of Guadalupe carried by Hidalgo's army now is a highlight of the Gallery of Mexican History, Chapultepec Park, Mexico City.

With more peasants and *criollos* flocking to the banner of Guadalupe with each passing day, the revolution began to seem unstoppable. Would even the well-armed soldiers of the capital dare to stand and fight such an angry horde? Surely not!

On to Guanajuato!

Juan Antonio Riaño, chief magistrate of Guanajuato, was a worried man. Running a wealthy city of 66,000 population was no small job. After all, Guanajuato was the third largest city in Spanish America; only Mexico City and Havana, Cuba, were larger. Riaño had done his job well for 18 years but now his proud city faced the greatest threat in its history.

Riaño had heard of *El Grito de Dolores* two days after it happened. He knew that the storm was blowing his way and would soon descend. How should he defend this key city in the Spanish empire?

Most of the city's buildings were in a long, narrow canyon. An attacking force had to be kept off the ridges overlooking the town. Once in control of those high places, the rebels could quickly make life impossible in Guanajuato. But in order to defend those dangerous ridges, Riaño would have to call on most of the town's population. The *gachupines* he could depend on, of course, and certainly some of the *criollos*. But many of the defenders would have to be *mestizos* and Indians. How many of these would fight? If not many, the enemy would soon come screaming into the town from the high places.

Riaño could not bring himself to trust the lower classes, so he chose Plan B. Near the center of town was a building used as a grain warehouse, the Alhóndiga. Its thick stone walls were four stories high; it was a natural fort. Stored in it was enough corn to support 500 persons for several months, if necessary.

Riaño did not think it would be necessary. Royalist troops would arrive within a few days to rescue Guanajuato. Surely a mighty building like the Alhóndiga could be held until then.

He ordered all government records and *gachupín* treasure moved into the Alhóndiga. After dark on September 24, *gachupines,* soldiers and some *criollos* closed themselves into their fortress . . . or tomb.

The lower classes now had no choice. Their magistrate had not only left them to the mercy of the onrushing rebels, he had taken away most of their food. The die was cast for the tragedy of Guanajuato, that long, livid scar on the history of Mexico. It happened on September 28.

DEATH TO GACHUPINES!

It was Father Hidalgo himself who led the first wave of rebels into the town. It was said that the rebels paused only long enough to rob a candy store before assaulting the Alhóndiga. The royalist street barricades simply melted before the angry mob.

If there ever was a chance for Hidalgo to control his troops, the chance was lost when the town's lower classes joined the rebels, screaming "Death to *gachupines!*" and stampeding toward the fortress.

From the roof and windows of the Alhóndiga, the royalists fired into the oncoming wall of human flesh. The rebel wounded were soon put out of their misery, trampled under the mad rush of those bringing up the rear.

Magistrate Riaño was killed early in the action. Captain Allende didn't show up until the battle was well underway. Had he appeared earlier, it might have been different . . . but history doesn't wait.

For a time it appeared that the attacking force might beat itself to death against the hard walls. It is said that stones thrown by attackers were piled a foot high on the roof of the Alhóndiga, but the fort still protected those huddled within.

Then someone had an idea. Stone walls won't burn, but wooden doors will. But how to get close enough to set the wood afire? A hail of death still poured down from the walls.

Then a young man of the town volunteered. His nickname was *"Pípila,"* or "Chicken Neck." Not too promising a start, one might say. It would have been better if his nickname had been *"Tortuga,"* or "Turtle," because a large, flat stone was strapped to his back.

Then *Pípila* grabbed a torch and scuttled toward the door. Guns blazed down from the walls; bullets bounced like hail off the stone. At last *Pípila* managed to set the door afire. Rebel shouts told the story. As soon as the flame licked up, the battle was as good as over.

When the door fell in flames, a howling mob stormed into the Alhóndiga, screaming, slashing, looting. It is believed that more than 300 persons died in the final assault. Unfortunately for Hidalgo's cause, not all the dead were *gachupines* and soldiers; some were *criollos*. The few Spaniards who were taken prisoner probably were saved only by the arrival of an angry Captain Allende.

The nightmare did not end with the fall of the fortress. Forty years later, the wild episode was described in a book by a man who watched it:

"Those who had surrendered begged on their knees for mercy but in vain . . . Most of the soldiers were killed; others took off their uniforms and escaped by mingling with the crowd. Perishing among the officers were many young men of the most distinguished families. Some tried to hide in Bin Number 21 with the dead bodies of the Intendant (Riaño) and others but they were found and slaughtered without mercy. All were stripped of their clothing. Those left alive were tied together and taken naked to the jail . . .

"The populace gave itself up to stealing everything that had been stored in the Alhóndiga and it was all gone in a few moments. The building was a most horrible spectacle. Food that had been stored was scattered all around; naked bodies lay buried in maize, or in money, and everything was splattered with blood . . .

"The citizens who had stayed on the ridges to await the outcome came down to take part in the looting . . . That afternoon and night and the following night they sacked all the shops and houses belonging to the Europeans. On that deadly night the scene was lighted by great numbers of torches, and nothing was heard but the noise of blows crashing against the doors and the ferocious howling of the rabble applauding their fall and

rushing in in triumph to remove goods, furniture and everything else."

Then Father Hidalgo called the madness to a halt. It is possible that he couldn't have stopped it sooner even if he had wanted to.

"If we continue as we did today," he is reported to have said on the night of the Alhóndiga's fall, "the victory is the work of but a few months."

But all was not rosy for the rebel cause. In fact, the seeds of defeat may have been planted on those terrible nights in Guanajuato. First, Hidalgo had hoped to use the *gachupín* riches in the Alhóndiga to finance the revolution. Instead, all but a few thousand *pesos* of it had slipped into the pockets of thieves.

Also, Hidalgo needed support of *criollos* but after their suffering in Guanajuato, he had little chance of getting it.

But at the moment, these things seemed unimportant. The rising cry was: "On to Mexico City! Death to *gachupines!*"

POWER OF THE PRESS

As the rebels advanced toward the capital, another kind of war opened up. The royalists won this war easily, because they had the only weapon that counted --- the printing press. The rebels had none.

Royalist printers saw to it that the horrors of Guanajuato were reported in all gory detail and distributed to *criollos*. The best the rebels could do was a few hand-lettered posters.

As the royalist printed matter pointed out, the war cry of the rebels was "Death to *gachupines!*" but in the heat of battle, Hidalgo's men had shown themselves eager to kill and rob *criollos*, too.

Frightened *criollos* wondered: if Hidalgo's revolt is nothing more than a riot of the lower class against the upper, where do we stand?

It was not too late for Hidalgo to change his approach. Captain Allende constantly urged him to take in more regular military units, then let untrained Indians go back to their homes. In other words, Allende wanted more of an army and less of a mob.

A peasant plows the Mexican soil in sight of a great mountain.

Hidalgo refused. What had begun as a peasant revolt would continue as a peasant revolt.

In the capital, Viceroy Venegas was bending before the storm. On October 5, 1810, he ordered that tribute payments --- hated by the lower classes --- be done away with. He even had the proclamation translated into Náhuatl, the widely-used Indian language.

The royalist moves may have worked. As Hidalgo's forces approached Mexico City, fewer recruits joined the crusade. But even so, there may have been as many as 80,000 persons following the banner of Guadalupe. By this time, even Father Hidalgo couldn't be sure of the numbers in his rag-tag band.

Against this mass of humanity, Royalist General Torcuato Trujillo could send only 2500 soldiers!

In late October, less than a month after *El Grito*, battle was joined at Monte de las Cruces, west of the capital. The record shows a victory for the rebels, because Trujillo was forced to order a retreat. But the royalist artillery, thundering and smoking and blasting huge holes in the rebel ranks, may have made its mark despite the "defeat." It was said that some Indians were so mystified by these terrible cannons that they rushed up to them and covered the muzzles with their hats!

Now Mexico City, ruling center of the hated *gachupines*, lay nearly defenseless before the Hidalgo forces. Final victory for the rebels seemed only days away. But then a strange thing happened . . .

Father Hidalgo did not order an attack. Something held him back. Days passed; Hidalgo and Allende argued. Allende demanded an immediate attack; Hidalgo refused.

True, their army had been hurt badly. Thousands had been killed or wounded; thousands more had deserted. But there were still tens of thousands ready to move into the capital. Why did Hidalgo hesitate?

Some suggest that Hidalgo was afraid to let his army enter Mexico City for fear that it would run wild again. Then, when General Calleja arrived with royalist rescue forces, he could cut the rebels to pieces.

For whatever reason, the Captain General of the Americas ordered his army to move west toward Guadalajara, away from the capital, on November 3.

There were more battles but they changed nothing. The arguments between Hidalgo and Allende continued; Hidalgo usually had his way. General Calleja was pursuing the rebels now; the two armies met at a bridge called Calderón.

The day ended in disgrace for the rebels, who lost 1200 dead. Calleja lost only 50. You could say that the Hidalgo revolt ended at Calderón, but the bloodshed continued.

One battle too late, the rebel forces set down Hidalgo and made Allende their military leader. But now the move could not save their cause.

Escape to the south had been cut off. There was nothing for Allende and Hidalgo to do but slog northward with the sad remains of their army, about 1000 men. It seemed possible that a few friends would pop up behind the rocks along the trails through the northern deserts.

Losers are always lonely; few friends appeared. In fact, friends had become enemies. On February 21, Allende and Hidalgo and their hungry army were captured by Colonel Ignacio Elizondo near Saltillo. Not too long before, Elizondo had been a rebel.

In Chihuahua, 320 kilometers to the north, the last chapter was written. Hidalgo and Allende were put on trial and of course were convicted.

Father Hidalgo once had a fine sense of humor. Possibly it stuck with him to the end. It was said that he smiled as he approached members of his firing squad, then reached into his pocket and gave them pieces of candy.

The royalists were not so forgiving. They cut off the heads of Hidalgo, Allende, Aldama and Jiménez. They carried the heads to Guanajuato and hung them in cages at the corners of the Alhóndiga. They left the heads there for 10 years, until they had wasted away to bone. Then, finally, Mexico broke its last bonds with Spain and the heads came down.

But the names are still there. And the bitter memories . . . some of those are still there.

Four months . . .

The echoes of *El Grito de Dolores* died in four months. Why? What was Father Hidalgo's big mistake?

Let's make a guess. His mistake was that he believed that the object of his revolution was to make a better life for the lower classes. The way to make this better life was to break away from Spain. The way to break away from Spain was to harness the anger of the lower classes. Let them fight for their own freedom.

Good idea. But *mestizos* and Indians weren't trained soldiers; they would be asked to fight trained soldiers. Hidalgo's heart ruled his mind. This cost him his head but probably earned him an everlasting place in Mexican history.

So the revolt failed. If it failed, why is so much made of it? Because once word got around that successful revolt was possible, the grip of Spain on Mexico grew slippery.

MORELOS THE MAGNIFICENT

There is a state in the highlands of Mexico called Morelos; its capital is a beautiful city called Morelia. The names come from another priest --- José María Morelos. Had Morelos been the parish priest at Dolores in 1810, the breakaway from Spain might have come 10 years sooner.

Father Morelos had joined Hidalgo in October, 1810, and had been sent south to recruit an army. He made mistakes but he learned from them. He also learned from the mistakes of Hidalgo.

He learned not to turn loose an untrained mob, as Hidalgo had done. Instead, he developed a guerrilla army, the first such fighting force in Mexico. They fought the same enemy but with different methods.

A fast-moving Morelos unit would strike at the royalists with a flashing blow, then vanish into the mountains. The trails were well-known by their leader, who had been a mule driver in his youth.

Poor General Calleja . . . he was the best officer the Spaniards had. But he had been given the almost impossible task of tracking down Morelos and his roving bands of troublemakers.

This statue of Father Morelos shows him almost as plump as he actually was. It is near the palace of Cortés in Cuernavaca.

He worked hard at it, but it took him four years to finish the job.

But Father Morelos was more than a soldier. He was a thinker who had a lot of ideas about what kind of government Mexico should have when the Spanish had been whipped. He even put together a constitution at Apatzingan in 1814 and formed a revolutionary government.

There were great military victories for the Morelos forces at Oaxaca and Acapulco. But then a great mistake was made: an attack was ordered on a royalist stronghold, Valladolid. The rebels were beaten so badly they never recovered. The final charge for the royalists was led by a young officer named Augustín de Iturbide, who would be heard from again. An important Morelos lieutenant, Father Mariano Matamoros, was captured and shot.

Valladolid was a disaster, pure and simple. The surprise defeat destroyed morale and left the army disorganized. Military command was taken from Morelos; the end was near.

The fleeing rebels were caught in the state of Guerrero on November 5, 1815. After fighting until the top officers of his government could escape, Morelos surrendered.

Still proud, still unyielding, Father Morelos was shot on December 22, 1815. Many times his followers had asked him to become a dictator; he had always refused, saying the only title he wanted was that of "servant of his country." There was to be no "Captain of the Americas" for him.

A great man was Morelos, one who clearly deserves his towering place in Mexican history.

When Morelos died, the rebel movement died with him. Scattered bands still demanded the attention of General Calleja from time to time but at last, after six years of bloodshed and destruction, Mexico could be called peaceful. Spain held onto its power over the bleeding country but two priests, Hidalgo and Morelos, had almost tipped over the crown.

Scars of war marked the land from end to end. But out of the war came an organization which would control Mexico for most of the next hundred years --- a professional army. Many of the footsoldiers were Indians and *mestizos*; most of the officers were *criollos*. *Criollos* had discovered they could lead troops just as well as *gachupines* could. Also, many of them found that they liked the military life, with its colorful uniforms and medals and booty. As an army officer, a young, ambitious *criollo* no longer had to feel like a second-class citizen.

And such power they had! A *criollo*-led army was to set up or topple (or both) every Mexican government for most of the next century, so many governments that most Mexicans stopped counting.

Independence finally came to Mexico on September 27, 1821, when Iturbide, the officer who had crushed Morelos, proclaimed the new empire of Mexico. In 1822, he became Emperor Augustín I.

But Mexicans who thought the suffering was over were in for a surprise.

They had only begun to suffer.

The famous mummies of Guanajuato, a prime tourist attraction, now are protected by glass cases. Once they were displayed like this. The theory is that chemicals in the soil left over from mining days prevented decomposition of the bodies.

FIVE

--- The United States War

"RUN, RUN, SANTY ANNY IS BEHIND YOU!"

On a map, the line is sharply drawn between the U.S. and Mexico. Maybe this is wrong; maybe that line separating Mexico from California, Arizona, New Mexico and Texas really ought to be fuzzy.

It was like that, you know, back in the days when all these states were a part of Mexico.

It began with Moses Austin, who asked the Spaniards then ruling Mexico for permission to settle 300 families from the Mississippi Valley in the area we now call Texas. Spanish Governor Martínez said *"Sí."*

And why not? The barren country badly needed settlers who would develop it. Moses Austin could be trusted. After all, he had already become a Spanish citizen when he settled in Louisiana, then owned by Spain. And under the agreement, all settlers would swear loyalty to Mexico. They also were to become Catholics if they weren't already and would pay taxes to Mexico.

Stephen Austin gives a land title to Texas colonists of 1882.

It sounded like a good arrangement for both sides. What could go wrong? Well . . . quite a few things, as it turned out.

Something must have gone wrong, because from the seed that was planted in 1820 by Moses Austin and Governor Martínez grew two terrible wars between the U.S. and Mexico. These wars left a bad taste in the mouths of Mexicans that poisons U.S.-Mexico relations even today.

Moses Austin died before he could lead settlers to Texas. His son, Stephen, then only 27 years old, took over and placed the 300 families on land along the Brazos, Colorado and Bernard rivers and in towns named San Felipe de Austin, San Antonio, Gonzales and (somebody had a sense of humor) Washington-on-the-Brazos.

TRIPLE TROUBLE

Some of the later settlers had no intention of being loyal to Mexico, which would lead to trouble. Some had no intention of becoming Catholics, which would lead to more trouble. Some had no intention of paying taxes and duties to Mexico even at the point of a gun, which would lead to war.

Were some of the first Texas settlers a pack of liars then? Well, that's strong talk. They probably were no better nor worse than other settlers who were starting to move west toward California and Oregon at the same time. Driven by a gnawing hunger for free land and a new life, some would have sworn loyalty to the devil himself to get them.

There was another problem. The Austin group had permission to settle but of those who came later, few bothered to ask if it was all right with Mexico. Of about 25,000 *gringos* estimated to be in Texas in 1830, many were illegal immigrants from the U.S. South. These illegal settlers had no interest in Mexico and things Mexican. They wanted only to bring in slaves, raise cattle and cotton and get rich.

Small wonder that back in Mexico City, officials were worried. The border line between Mexican Texas and the U.S. was becoming too fuzzy for comfort. The 4000 Mexicans living in Texas were in danger of being drowned in a flood of Yankees. There was much talk in the *gringo* capital of something called "Manifest Destiny." There were those high in government who actually believed that God Himself wanted the U.S. to swallow up Texas and the West! Or so they said . . .

Mexico, you might remember, had declared itself independent of Spain in 1821, only one year before Stephen Austin started his settlement in Texas.

But in gaining freedom from European power, Mexico lost something, too. The Spanish had wiped out the old Indian nations in Mexico and most of the Indians, too. With the Indians went the old laws and customs governing human affairs. Then, for three centuries, the Spanish had tied the country tight with Spanish law, enforced by Spanish arms.

With both forms of government blown away on the wind, it is hardly surprising that trouble bubbled and boiled throughout Mexico. For a long time to come, Mexico would be ruled by *caudillos* --- military dictators. A *caudillo* could hold power only as long as he could pay his soldiers, the strong right arm of his power.

There were many *caudillos* in Mexico after 1821. Sometimes a *caudillo* stayed in control for only a few days; one who held power for six months was considered a grand old man of government. A name has been given to this wild form of non-government: *santanismo*. The name comes from that of Antonio López de Santa Anna, one of the most fantastic rascals ever to march through the cluttered halls of world history.

It was Santa Anna who would play the lead role in the U.S. War. It was "Ol' Santy Anny," as some Texans referred to him, who was to come down through Texas history as Satan himself. Santy Anny, some said, was a man totally without honor, a lying, thieving skunk and a scoundrel besides. And this was on his good days . . .

And before Santa Anna was kicked out of office for the last time, there were Mexicans who would use those same words about him . . . and add a few juicy Spanish terms.

SANTA ANNA MAKES HIS MOVE

After operating behind the scenes for years, Santa Anna became president of Mexico in 1833. A year later, he felt powerful enough to declare himself dictator. To nail down his control,

A typical house along the U.S.-Mexico border in the old days had adobe walls and a thatched roof. Yes, it probably leaked a little.

he needed a great military victory over one of Mexico's swarming enemies. Or, Santa Anna being Santa Anna, a small victory in a distant place would do. When Santa Anna blew his own trumpet, truth was usually drowned out in the first blast.

His crafty eyes searched the scene for an easy victim. Why not Texas? Mexicans had been complaining for years about how Texas was filling up with crude Yankee immigrants, legal and illegal. They weren't paying their taxes up there. They were calling Mexicans "greasers." To top it all off, a loud Texas politician named Sam Houston had been bold enough to bellow in public against the dictatorship of Santa Anna.

Santa Anna was 53 years old when he set out on his Texas adventure. As always, he showed the energy of a much younger man and the nerve of a pirate. One long arm reached out to grab several thousand recruits for his army, the other borrowed money from loan sharks (the national treasury was broke, as usual) for munitions and carts and horses. Before long he had an army of sorts put together at San Luis Potosí. Then, with the winds of winter whipping around his ears, he drove his army toward San Antonio, Texas, a grim 1000 kilometers to the north.

Toward a fort called "Alamo," thus setting the stage for one of the most famous battles of U.S. history.

The red-letter date in Texas history is March 6, 1836 --- Alamo Day. Four days earlier a convention at Washington-on-the-Brazos had declared Texas independent from Mexico. A constitution had been adopted. Colonel Sam Houston was named commander-in-chief of the Texas army, such as it was.

In an old mission near San Antonio that had been converted into a fort, less than 200 Texans under Lieutenant Colonel William Barret Travis had decided to make a stand. It was rumored that Santa Anna's army numbered as high as 6000 men! But if the Texans could hold out for just a short time, Travis thought, help would arrive. If the Alamo and San Antonio fell, Travis feared, the Texan cause would be lost.

Help did not arrive. Santa Anna did. The Mexican army did not number 6000 as had been rumored, but only 2000 or so; many of these were half-starved and crippled by disease.

The main building of the Alamo as it looks today, photographed from a gate into the adjoining walled courtyard.

This engraving shows the action at the battle of Alamo centering on the walled courtyard next to the main building. The reason was simple: the main church building is fairly small and couldn't hold all the defenders. Also, there weren't enough openings to shoot from.

Cannon roared inside and outside the Alamo. Rifles and pistols blasted away at close range. Smoke drifted across the nightmare scene as men screamed and died. At the last, as Mexicans began to pour through the gashes in the adobe walls, crying "Death to *gringos!*", swords flashed in the smoke and dust. Blood soaked the soil of the Alamo.

Once inside, they battled for an hour. Among those who died were two famous frontiersmen, Davy Crockett and Jim Bowie. Crockett died fighting, the legend says, while Bowie, very ill at the time, was killed in bed.

Not all who died in the Alamo were *gringos*. There were also native-born Mexicans fighting for the Texas cause. One of these was a *criollo*, Juan Seguin, who survived only because he had been sent on a dangerous mission in search of help.

HORROR AT GOLIAD

And so, it was a great victory for Santa Anna. Or was it? He must have thought so on March 6. Puffed up with his triumph, he sent a harsh order to another Mexican officer who had captured the entire Texas garrison of 380 persons at Goliad: "Kill all the prisoners."

It was done. In the smoke drifting away from the Alamo, in the winds blowing across the slaughter ground at Goliad, there were messages which would soon turn into angry battle cries:

"REMEMBER THE ALAMO! REMEMBER GOLIAD!"

(At this point someone probably ought to say a quiet word on behalf of Antonio López de Santa Anna. He had learned his rules of war in the Mexican struggle for independence from Spain. In those wars, it was the habit to take no prisoners. Also, one wonders if Santa Anna's forces in Texas could have handled large numbers of prisoners. The Mexicans themselves were half-starved, remember. And just disarming the Texans and turning them loose would have been very dangerous. As soon as the Texans found more guns, they would surely point them at Santa Anna's rear. One thousand kilometers from his home base, always short of ammunition and other supplies, Santa Anna

This is how General Santa Anna looked to an artist during the prime of his life, if he had one. It is believed that Santa Anna's often weird behavior grew out of his dope addiction. He had a fondness for opium, in particular.

probably couldn't have done anything but wipe out the prisoners. He has been called a lot of names, most of them true, but nobody ever called him dumb. As it turned out, slaughtering the prisoners angered the Texans so much that it led directly to the defeat of Santa Anna and the loss of Texas. One wonders if the clever old rascal worried about that when he made the decision.)

Many Texans were frightened by reports of Santa Anna's approach. They urged Sam Houston, commander of the small Texas army, to march out to meet the Mexican forces.

Houston had other ideas. He ordered the Texas army to retreat toward Louisiana. His plan, which he kept to himself, was to put off another battle until the situation was right. He wanted no more massacres.

But the Texans wanted to fight, not run, so they left Houston's army in droves and went home to protect their families.

The early battles between the Texans and the Mexicans only seemed to build Santa Anna's confidence. He began to feel that he could whip these Texans almost any time he wanted to.

Santa Anna's feeling about Texas troops was shared by settlers watching Houston's retreating soldiers.

"Run, run, Santy Anny is behind you!" cried old ladies from their doorsteps.

Santa Anna, smelling final victory, pushed his army harder than ever. After a forced march of 64 kilometers in a single day, his army swooped down on Harrisburg and took it without firing a shot.

It was enough to make a soldier angry. As the full story of Santa Anna's brutality at the Alamo and at Goliad spread through the ranks, it was enough to make a soldier more angry. Here, staring into the campfire, was one whose friend had died at the Alamo; here was another whose relative had perished at Goliad.

Finally Sam Houston said, "The army will cross and we will meet the enemy. Some of us may be killed and will be killed; but, soldiers, remember the Alamo, the Alamo! The Alamo!"

On April 21 at San Jacinto, in little more than 15 minutes of hard fighting, General Sam Houston and his Texas army

wiped out the Mexican force, killing 400, wounding 200 and taking 730 prisoners!

History has a way of playing little jokes and this was one of them. The Texans were so short of ammunition as they approached San Jacinto that they had to load their cannons with broken horseshoes. So how did Houston's forces manage to make such quick work of dumping Santa Anna off his high horse? Simple. They caught the Mexican general and his army taking their siesta!

With the battle going badly, Santa Anna grabbed a horse, leaped aboard and galloped off. Knowing that he would soon be recognized in his gaudy uniform, he put on dirty old clothes stolen from a hut. (Some say women's clothes.) Captured by the Texans but unrecognized, Santa Anna was brought into camp, where there were other Mexican prisoners. He might have fooled the Texans but he couldn't fool his own soldiers. They SALUTED their commanding officer!

There was talk of shooting Ol' Santy Anny. Others objected; hang him, they said, and save the ammunition.

But Santa Anna, who could bargain his way out of a den of starving wolves, talked himself out of this scrape, too. All he did was promise Sam Houston that Mexico would recognize the independence of Texas. Mexico didn't, but Santa Anna returned to Mexico, where he told one and all about his glorious victories in Texas. He probably didn't think to mention San Jacinto.

THE MOST WICKED WAR

Santa Anna's war was small potatoes; much worse was on the way. Ten years later, Mexico and the U.S. would be involved in a ruckus about which Civil War General U. S. Grant would say, "I do not think there was ever a more wicked war than that waged by the United States on Mexico."

The seed of the terrible war was planted in Texas but the crop would be harvested also in Arizona, New Mexico and California.

Texas, having chased Santa Anna back to Mexico, was ready to look northeast, to Washington, D. C. Politicians in Washington looked the other way, at first. The problem was black slavery, which was fairly common in Texas. Politicians from free states refused to admit Texas to the Union as a slave state; Texans refused to give up their slaves.

So, in 1836, Texans formed their own republic with Sam Houston as first elected president.

The Texas Republic really didn't work very well, but then, nobody expected it to. Within a few years, the government was deep in debt. The second president, Mirabeau Lamar, had taken in money with a spoon and put it out with a shovel. Texans continued to ask the U.S. to take them under its wing but got nowhere. Then Sam Houston hinted that if the U.S. wasn't interested, Great Britain might be.

At which point the U.S. decided that Texas might be squeezed into the Union after all. Late in 1845, Texas became a part of the United States of America.

To no one's surprise, the Mexican government was furious. Apparently Santa Anna was the only Mexican who recognized the independence of Texas. Mexico broke off relations with the U.S. in January, 1846. The Mexican ambassador sailed for home, muttering about *"gringo* thievery."

Thus the stage was set for a war which Mexico had no chance to win. Before it was over, Mexico would suffer a great humiliation which still stings: the sight of *gringo* troops clattering over the cobblestones of Mexico City, ancient capital of a proud land.

And in the final moments of the city's agony, children would fight and die in the hopeless cause.

General Zachary Taylor, rough as a cob, was sent south by U.S. President Polk to knock some Yankee sense into the heads of Mexicans. (Among those who strongly opposed the war, incidentally, was a young Illinois congressman of whom you may have heard: Abraham Lincoln.)

Then, in Mexico, a very interesting thing happened . . .

The Yankees were blockading the port of Veracruz. No one entered Mexico through that particular door unless the U.S.

Some Texans lived better than others. This handsome casa was the home of José Policarpo Rodríguez and family. Location: Privilege Creek, near Bandera, Texas.

said so. But a certain Mexican was allowed to slip through. Who else but Antonio López de Santa Anna, returned again from exile just in the nick of time?

Mexico City was in an uproar. The money cupboard was nearly bare. With war looming against the so-called "Colossus of the North," only 1839 *pesos* remained in the treasury! The army was in such bad shape that it contained more officers than men, 24,000 to 20,000. The people were rising in anger, with good reason.

Santa Anna to the rescue! Wearing civilian clothes, the rascal was driven in an ordinary buggy through the streets of Mexico City, then was talked into accepting the presidency --- again --- in this great hour of need.

Working furiously at what he did best --- organizing --- Santa Anna whipped together an army of 18,000 men. He pushed this army north, again from San Luis Potosí, but lost 4000 soldiers along the way. Some just walked off, some died of disease, others just plain starved.

But the day came at Buena Vista in northern Mexico when Santa Anna's skinny, hungry Mexicans fought the Yankee army of Zachary Taylor to a standstill. It was Mexican bayonets in the hands of brave men against Yankee big guns. Santa Anna's soldiers won many small victories but were finally cut to pieces by Taylor's artillery.

After the loss of 1500 dead and wounded, Santa Anna took advantage of a sudden storm which stopped the battle, then slipped away under cover of darkness. Taylor's army was too exhausted to follow.

The Mexican army which straggled into San Luis Potosí 17 days later was made up mostly of barefoot skeletons. It had given Taylor's Yankees all the fight they could handle but it had paid a bloody price.

The battle of Buena Vista may have taken most of the fight out of Santa Anna, too, as we shall see.

SCOTT'S MAD MISSION

Discouraged and disgusted by the defeat in the north, many Mexicans were almost relieved to hear that the Yankees were coming at them from another direction. General Winfield

Scott and 10,000 troops had landed at Veracruz and were marching toward Mexico City!

The rag-tag remnants of Santa Anna's northern army put up a fight of sorts at Cerro Gordo; the Yankees brushed them aside. Santa Anna was still in charge but this was not the old Santa Anna, the terror of Texas.

General Scott should never have reached Mexico City to deliver his historic slap-in-the-face to Mexican honor. If Santa Anna and his soldiers had fought as well in defense of their capital as they had fought at Buena Vista, the Yankees would have been crushed.

After all, Scott had only 10,000 troops. That many Mexican soldiers could have been enlisted in Mexico City alone. Besides, Scott's supply lines stretched 483 kilometers back to Veracruz, a dangerous situation for any invading army. Even worse, Scott had no troops in reserve. All things considered, Scott's invasion of Mexico was one of history's most foolish campaigns --- but it worked.

It worked because Santa Anna, always the peacock, refused to share any glory with General Gabriel Valencia, who now commanded the northern division. When the Mexican armies were in position for the defense of the capital, Santa Anna ordered Valencia to withdraw!

Valencia was furious, called Santa Anna a coward and refused to obey the order.

So Santa Anna snorted, pulled out his own soldiers and left Valencia --- and Mexico City --- to their shameful fate.

SIX BOYS, SIX HEROES

At the lower end of Chapultepec Park in modern Mexico City, a great monument attracts the eyes of the thousands who pass it each day. There are six tall, white columns defying a smoggy sky, decorated near the top with black eagles.

Each column represents a Mexican boy: Juan de la Barrera, Francisco Márquez, Fernando Montes de Oca, Agustín Melgar, Vicente Suárez and Juan Escutia.

These six teenagers were attending the military college on Chapultepec Hill, a strongpoint overlooking the city. When church bells rang to announce the approach of General Scott's

The storming of Chapultepec Castle by troops of General Scott is depicted in the heroic style of the day.

Yankees, the military cadets could have fled with Santa Anna's soldiers. But they chose to stay and fight --- and thus became actors in a dramatic legend learned early by every Mexican school child. History knows them now as *Los Niños Heroes*, the Boy Heroes.

The mists of history surround *Los Niños Heroes*, fogging the facts. What is known is that they were on the hill when Scott's forces attacked, that they fought bravely, that they refused to surrender.

One story says that a boy wrapped himself in the Mexican flag, then threw himself off the wall surrounding Chapultepec Castle. When General Scott saw the broken body, it is said, he realized that he was fighting boys, not men, and called off the attack.

Another story insists that all six boys wrapped themselves in flags and threw themselves off the wall.

Still another account relates that the six boys killed themselves rather than surrender, shouting *"Viva Mexico! Viva Colegio Militar!"* as they died.

Maybe, in this case, details aren't important. What is known for sure is that the boys did fight against the Yankee invaders and died proudly in a war which left little pride for anyone, Mexican or *gringo*.

The monument honoring *Los Niños Heroes* in Mexico City is a national shrine; there are other monuments outside of the capital. Many streets in Mexican cities and towns are named *"Los Niños Heroes"*; the name lives throughout the country in honor of the gallant young defenders of Chapultepec Castle.

This most wicked of all wars ended with the Treaty of Guadalupe Hidalgo. With General Scott's guns still pointed at their heads, Mexico's leaders, weak and disorganized, gave up over half of Mexico's territory to the U.S. for a mere 15 million dollars! Included was the last Mexican claim to Texas and much of what is now Arizona, New Mexico and California.

Thus ended the first U.S. war ever to be fought entirely on foreign soil.

Los Niños Heroes were in the news again in March, 1947, both in the U.S. and in Mexico. A U.S. president, Harry Truman, was visiting Mexico at the invitation of Mexican President Miguel Alemán.

President Truman had been warned that his reception by the Mexican people might be cold. Instead it was warm and friendly. So in the afternoon, President Truman got an idea: he would go to Chapultepec Park, to the *Los Niños Heroes* monument.

The people around Truman argued against the notion. They told the president that Mexicans would be reminded of the wicked war and would be angry. They said also that Texans would be annoyed and wouldn't support him in the future.

President Truman thought it over, then said, "Any Texan that's fool enough to be put out when a president of the United States pays tribute to a bunch of brave kids, I don't need their support."

So Truman went to the monument and laid a wreath upon it and bowed his head in tribute.

It is said that young Mexican soldiers at the scene burst into tears.

Perhaps the wounds of the most wicked of wars finally began to heal on that day in March, 1947.

➡

These six columns in Mexico City's Chapultepec Park were erected near the spot where Los Niños Heroes made their stand.

SIX

--- The Years of Reform

ENTER THE BAREFOOT BOY

A strange thing happened in Mexico City on January 11, 1861: a new president was put into office.

What's so strange about that, you ask? Good question. After all, Mexico had been changing leaders with each new season --- or so it seemed. Dressed in gaudy uniforms of red, blue and gold, riding in fancy, gilded carriages, escorted by thousands of prancing soldiers, the new rulers of the bleeding land always had played the role of conquering commander-in-chief. Bands played; banners fluttered; cheering crowds lined the parade route as *El Presidente* rolled toward the National Palace on the Zócalo.

And that's what was different about January 11, 1861. The new president was not dressed in a uniform, but in a plain black suit. His carriage was black, too, and just as plain as his suit. He carried no sword at his side. Inside the carriage, the president sat quietly, not waving, not smiling, only leaning

slightly forward in his seat. There was no celebration; none had been ordered.

On that day in 1861, Mexico was getting its first civilian president. It was also getting its greatest national hero, although who could have guessed that then? This short, plump, homely man with the dark, rugged face of his Indian ancestors was Benito Juárez. A name the world would remember . . .

He was a man of law, come to lead a nation torn apart by lawlessness. He was a man of peace in a nation which had seen little but war.

Sometimes Juárez is referred to as "Mexico's Abraham Lincoln."

Mexicans can be forgiven if they look at it differently. They might think of Lincoln as the U.S.'s Benito Juárez.

In the game of history, luck often plays a part. A certain person is in a certain place at a certain time. For instance, it is possible that Mexico gained its greatest hero because a sheep was stolen. Hear the story, then judge for yourself.

One of the most beautiful states of Mexico is Oaxaca, far to the south. Its low, green mountains and well-watered valleys were part of the estate granted to Hernán Cortés by the Spanish crown.

In this area, in December of 1818, a 12-year-old boy of the Zapotec Indian tribe was tending his uncle's sheep. The sheep were precious to his uncle, so tending them was a responsible job. But it was not terribly exciting. So when a band of mule drivers halted for a rest nearby, the boy fell into eager conversation with them.

What tales they told this country boy of life in the city of Oaxaca! But only too soon, the mule drivers moved on. Returning to duty, the boy counted sheep.

One was missing!

Many years later, the boy wrote of the incident: "Another boy, a much older boy, approached me and seeing my grief told

The only note of humor, if it can be called that, in the Juárez Museum in the National Palace is this drawing by a cartoonist of the day. Note plain black coach in background.

me that he had seen one of the mule drivers make away with the sheep while the others held my attention."

Fearing his uncle's wrath, the crying boy hurried down the mountainside toward the city of Oaxaca. The date was December 17, 1818; the boy was Benito Juárez.

It was not a promising beginning, perhaps, but had Juárez been a better sheepherder, Mexico might never have heard of him. He might well have lived out his life in his native mountains.

Young Benito was not entirely alone in Oaxaca. His sister worked there as a cook for the family of Antonio Mazza. Soon a job was found for Benito with Don Antonio Salanueva, a bookbinder. Now the world began to open up for the Indian boy from the mountains, who could not even speak Spanish. Don Antonio, who in time became the boy's godfather, taught him more than language; he told young Benito about Hidalgo and Morelos and other heroes of the struggle for independence.

The time was right for Benito Juárez. When Mexico finally broke away from Spain in 1821, a new school was opened in Oaxaca. The old schools had been controlled by the church or by the wealthy class; the new one allowed students to think for themselves. Young Benito did a lot of thinking; he also learned to read and write in Spanish and began serious study of the law. Then luck again pointed a finger . . .

THAT FAMILIAR FACE

Excitement stirred the Institute in Oaxaca in 1829. None other than the great General Antonio López de Santa Anna was coming to town. It was decided to honor His Majesty with a dinner at the Institute.

The general's waiter, as luck would have it, was a stocky, barefoot, young Indian. Santa Anna took pains to find out the waiter's name. It was Benito Juárez.

In time, these two men would become bitter enemies; their historic clashes would echo throughout Mexico. Santa Anna went to his grave believing that Juárez had hated him ever since that night in Oaxaca. Santa Anna, the pampered guest, dressed in his splendid best; Juárez, the servant, without even shoes. . .

One thing we know: Juárez understood about clothes and the message they carry. A few years after the Santa Anna banquet, he adopted the costume which would be his trade mark until the end of his life --- a black suit, a white shirt (handmade by his wife), a black bow tie. And black shoes . . .

Although he became a Mexican, Juárez remained a Zapotec. In 1848, after a term in the national congress, the widely respected Juárez was elected governor of the state of Oaxaca. Out of the mountains walked the friends of his Zapotec boyhood, bringing him gifts of pottery and serapes, sometimes sleeping in the halls of the governor's mansion.

Governor Juárez built roads and schools but still managed to balance the budget. Well ahead of his time, he favored the education of women.

But Oaxaca was a part of Mexico and Mexico was having its problems. Yankee generals Taylor and Scott had defeated Mexican armies under Santa Anna, who ran like a thief. Of course he did. He had Texas Rangers on his trail bellowing, "Remember the Alamo!"

Santa Anna felt that the safest place to run to was Oaxaca. It was not the best choice.

"Sorry, General," said Juárez, quietly but firmly. "There is no place for you here."

Insulted and enraged, Santa Anna left the country again.

Possibly Juárez could have made no other decision. He knew that if he accepted Santa Anna, the Yankees would invade his beloved Oaxaca. He also knew that allowing a troublemaker like Santa Anna to remain in Mexico was like keeping a fox in a chickenhouse.

General Santa Anna had a long memory. When he came back to power, as he always seemed to, he would remember Benito Juárez.

JUAREZ, THE CIGAR MAKER

Benito Juárez finished his term as governor, then began a quiet life of law practice in Oaxaca. But on May 27, 1853, everything fell apart.

The island prison of San Juan de Ulúa, the dank sweatbox which held Benito Juárez and many other famous prisoners. Now, as a national historic monument, it can be toured. The city of Veracruz is in background.

To no one's surprise, Santa Anna had been called back to rule Mexico. One of his first moves as president was to send his son to Oaxaca to arrest 47-year-old Benito Juárez.

Before May 27, 1853, the date of his arrest, Juárez hadn't cared for Santa Anna; that was plain enough. But after that date, the Zapotec hated Santa Anna and all he stood for. The barefoot boy and simple country lawyer was about to be turned into a firebrand of revolution. Arresting Juárez turned out to be one of Santa Anna's worst mistakes.

For 75 days, Juárez was jailed without visitors in Jalapa, near Veracruz. Seventy-five days --- two and one-half months. Nothing to do but think. Then he was taken to Veracruz and thrown into a stinking stone pile, the famous offshore fortress of San Juan de Ulúa. He had to suffer this for only 12 days, after which he was put aboard a ship bound for England.

Juárez had no money to pay for passage, so the captain kicked him off at the ship's first stop, Havana, Cuba. He knew where he wanted to go --- the U.S. --- and managed to get to New Orleans. There he joined other Mexicans who had been forced to flee the anger of Santa Anna.

Juárez worked as a cigar maker to earn a living; his wife helped by getting a job in Mexico. But Juárez was making more than cigars; he was making a revolution.

In the state of Guerrero in southwest Mexico, revolt against Santa Anna had already broken out. Its leader: Juan Alvarez, a skilled guerrilla fighter. In the U.S., Juárez and his group of plotters did what they could for Alvarez. They begged weapons and ammunition from the U.S. government and smuggled them to Alvarez. The guerrilla fighter welcomed advice, too, since he felt uncomfortable in the role of political leader.

In March, 1854, Alvarez was joined in Guerrero by Ignacio Comonfort, another foe of Santa Anna. There they published the Plan of Ayutla, which demanded a new government and constitution.

So Santa Anna put on his fanciest uniform and marched out from the capital to destroy his enemies. He ran into a small problem, though --- he couldn't find anybody. The wily Alvarez knew all the hiding places in Guerrero. But Santa Anna knew exactly what to do; he'd done it before. He trotted back into Mexico City and announced, in effect, "Here I am, *amigos*, the winner! I've destroyed the enemies of Mexico again!"

It was nonsense and nobody knew it better than Santa Anna. There was another problem, too: the money cupboard was bare again. Santa Anna had an idea about that. He would simply sell another chunk of his motherland to the U.S. It was done; the Mesilla valley became part of Arizona. Price: 10 million dollars. Some of the money went to pay Santa Anna's soldiers and bureaucrats; some, it was whispered, went into Santa Anna's personal bank accounts in other countries.

RETURN OF JUAREZ

The spring season in 1855 brought the sprouting of revolutionary seeds in northern Mexico; many officials there announced their support of the Plan of Ayutla. Then, in July, a squat, homely figure stepped off a boat in Acapulco --- Benito Juárez.

Santa Anna got the message. In August, he ran off to his estate in Venezuela, leaving his country in an uproar. Bankrupt, too, of course. The country, that is, not Santa Anna.

(Santa Anna should not be allowed to gallop off history's stage without a salute, of sorts. He may have been the only political hero who ever rode into power on one leg . . . a leg he didn't have. In 1838, a French fleet blockaded Veracruz. A landing party caught Santa Anna asleep and he was forced to escape in his underwear. The French went back to their ships but Santa Anna had no intention of letting them get off so easily. He mounted his white horse and charged; a French cannon ball took off his leg below the knee. He thought he was dying and dictated a final message to his countrymen which ended like this: "I also beg of the government of the fatherland to bury me in these same sand dunes, so that my companions in arms may know that this is the battle line I have marked out for them to hold." Santa Anna, recovered, loved his missing leg much more than he loved his remaining one. In 1842, after Santa Anna had been coaxed into ruling Mexico one more time, that lost leg --- or what remained of it --- was dug up on Santa Anna's estate

The real support for Benito Juárez came from villages like this one, El Abra. These thatched cottages, with walls (if any) made of thin stakes, very well suited the needs of the mild climate. There probably wasn't a mortgage on a single one of the simple dwellings. Villages much like this can still be seen in rural Mexico. For that matter, this picture isn't ancient; note railroad car and tracks in background.

and brought to Mexico City! Then, with proper ceremony, it was buried in the cemetery of Santa Paula. There were speeches and poems and cannon salutes. Santa Anna felt so good about it that he put on a new cork leg for his appearance at the ceremony. In 1853, Santa Anna took office for the eleventh and last time. He stayed in power until 1855, when he was forced once again to run for cover. He was not allowed back into Mexico for 17 years. Then, as a very old man, he came home to the land he had served so badly. No one cared about him any more, nor about his leg. In 1876, he performed his greatest service to his country by dying.)

In November, escorted by Indian warriors, Benito Juárez and his friends Comonfort and Alvarez rode into Mexico City to take over an impossible mess. (Santa Anna had a habit of leaving these behind him.) But Juárez, the man of law, knew what he had to do.

Under the old system, powerful church officials and army officers didn't have to worry about the legal system; that was for the peons. When charged with crimes, their trials were held in military or church courts. What it boiled down to was that these fat cats could get away with murder --- and sometimes did.

Juárez wiped out these privileges with one stroke of his pen. Named minister of justice in the Alvarez government, he immediately issued the Law of Juárez. Under it, army officers and churchmen would have to face the music in regular courts.

Juárez was soon to get more power. President Alvarez, the field soldier, was not comfortable at a desk in the National Palace; he wanted to return to the campfires of his compadres in Guerrero. He rode off into the sunset.

Comonfort took over as president. Benito Juárez became supreme court president and vice-president of the nation.

The *Ley Lerdo* --- Law of Lerdo --- was issued and it was a blockbuster. The intention was land reform, to distribute land to the peasants, the *campesinos*. Under *Ley Lerdo*, the Catholic church could no longer own land. What land it owned --- meaning a large chunk of what was left of Mexico after Santa Anna's wheeling and dealing --- would be sold. A high tax had to be paid to the government on each sale. No businesses nor organizations could own land, either. It was all supposed to be divided among the peasants.

A noble idea, but it didn't work.

Peasants couldn't buy land because there was no provision for breaking it up into small parcels and they couldn't afford large parcels. So who bought the land? Foreigners, mostly.

Many Indians farmed land owned by the community. Under the new law, these lands also had to be sold to private owners. Result? Hungry, out-of-work Indians. Angry, rioting Indians . . . trouble, trouble on every side.

Too far, too fast.

But any Mexican government in those years had to move fast. Great problems screamed for attention on all sides. With little money in the treasury, with a very thin base of support, it would have been foolish for a government, liberal or conservative, to put out a Ten Year Plan. "Action Now!" had to be the slogan, because tomorrow somebody else might hold the keys to the National Palace.

And so the liberals in 1857 put forth a new constitution which tried to do too much and do it too quickly. Frightened out of their wits by the far-reaching reforms, the conservatives cut and slashed even harder at the Comonfort government.

Finally Comonfort had to run into exile. Juárez was arrested but managed to escape.

Riding in his plain black coach, alone and unguarded, Juárez travelled the lonely trails of Mexico, meeting his people and talking, asking them to keep the faith just a little longer.

After a clearcut military victory in a battle near Mexico City, Juárez was able to move back into the palace. Elected to the presidency in March, 1860, he faced enormous problems.

That fluttering, squawking noise on the palace roof was made by more of Santa Anna's chickens coming home to roost. Much money had been borrowed from European countries to keep the Mexican economy afloat. Now Spain, England and France had grown tired of waiting for payment.

At the battle of Puebla, the Mexicans defending Fort Guadalupe meant business. It's hard to see how any army could fight in the white bloomers the French soldiers had to wear in those days. If the enemy was angry enough to THROW cannon balls at them, perhaps it didn't matter, anyway.

As newly-elected president, Juárez said, in effect, "Yes, Mexico owes you the money but *lo siento*. There is no way that Mexico can pay you."

Thus was set the stage for one of history's most outrageous episodes --- the establishment of a European-style monarchy in Mexico.

NAPOLEON GETS SNEAKY

It began innocently enough. England, France and Spain decided (and the Pope of Rome said it would be all right) to take Veracruz by force, then collect customs duties until Mexico's debts had been paid. A neat little plan . . .

But Napoleon III of France (nephew of the REAL Napoleon) had another plan, which he kept to himself. Mexican exiles in France had told him that the Mexican people were fed up with greedy dictators like Santa Anna and crude, fuzzy-minded "liberals" like Benito Juárez. What the people of Mexico really wanted, the exiles said, was a cozy little monarchy like that of France.

But would the U.S. allow this? After all, the *gringos* had marched into Mexico City in 1847; they worried about what happened in Mexico. Besides, Benito Juárez and the U.S. president, Abraham Lincoln, were known to be friends. Would Lincoln look away as French soldiers trampled Juárez into the dust?

Well . . . he just might have to. The U.S. was about to plunge into a bloody civil war. Lincoln's hands would be tied by problems at home.

Which is almost the way it worked out.

The French army landed at Veracruz, then eagerly marched inland, swatting mosquitoes as it left the swampy lowlands. But a funny thing happened on the way to Mexico City . . .

Napoleon had been told that Benito Juárez had no real support, that he ruled by fear. The *Juaristas* were said to be killers and robbers drawn from the lowest class of Mexican society. Under attack, *Juarista* forces would crumble and run like the *bandidos* they were.

The Abraham Lincoln of Mexico, Benito Juárez. Unlike Porfirio Díaz, Juárez never lost his Indian look, nor tried to.

So, on May 5, 1862, the cocky French army faced up to the *Juaristas* at Puebla. What the French managed to do was add a great national holiday to the Mexican calendar --- *Cinco de Mayo*. The French army stormed the fort of Loreto and got knocked on its rump.

Juarista General Ignacio Zaragoza and his Mexican army threw the proud French back toward the sea. A thousand French soldiers were lost.

It was a noble victory, one which shook up Napoleon. But *Cinco de Mayo* was only a battle, not a war. More French troops --- 30,000 of them --- were thrown into Mexico. At last, Mexican troops at the Puebla forts weren't beaten; they were simply starved out.

On June 10, 1863, French General Forey clattered into Mexico City.

Benito Juárez, too, had lost a battle but not a war. He retreated north to San Luis Potosí with his cabinet and the limping remains of his army.

On the morning of July 15, 1867, a familiar black coach rolled into Mexico City. Occupant: Benito Juárez. The French had been driven out but the Mexican president still was not smiling. He knew that the problems facing Mexico were greater than ever.

So Juárez acted quickly. One of his first moves was to dismiss two-thirds of the entire army!

The army was shocked at first, then grew bitter. Was this the thanks soldiers were to get for ten years of fighting and dying? And what were they supposed to do now, starve in the streets?

It was a bold, dangerous move by Juárez, a move that had to be made. Over the years, many Mexican generals had molded the soldiers under them into personal armies. The first loyalty of these soldiers was not to Mexico but to their own generals. Juárez knew that there could never be stable government or rule of law so long as this situation existed. It was time to end *caudillo* rule in Mexico.

The next years were hard times for Juárez and the country. But then, neither was used to easy times. Bankrupt, unable to trade with Europe because of the old debts, Mexico put aside fear of land-hungry *gringos* and turned to trade with the U.S. The Mexican countryside swarmed with *bandidos*, many of them unemployed soldiers trying to survive. A terrible drought in 1869 wiped out the harvest. Juárez could do almost nothing to help the starving.

Somehow, though, with all these problems, the government survived. Without much question, it was the beloved president himself who kept the lid from flying off. Mexico was not yet a country ruled by fair, honest laws, but the foundation had been built. Built almost entirely by one man . . .

Juárez was re-elected president in 1871. A disappointed general from Oaxaca, Porfirio Díaz, tried to lead a revolt against Juárez, but the uprising only sputtered, then died. The Juárez era was coming to an end, though; an enemy stronger than Santa Anna, stronger than Napoleon, stronger than Díaz, was knocking at the door.

Juárez had always been proud of his sturdy body and of his ability to withstand hardship. They could chase him around the mountain trails, they could throw him into prison, they could throw dirt on his ideas . . . but they could not defeat him. But the agony of Mexico had been the agony of Juárez, too. The years of suffering had taken their toll.

Soon after his 64th birthday in 1870, he had been ill but he had recovered. He took a great blow in 1871 when his wife died. She had been with him since the early days in Oaxaca; in fact, she was a member of one of the first families to befriend him when he came out of the mountains as a barefoot boy.

Heart attacks struck at him in July, 1872. Juárez refused to give in. On at least two occasions, attacks occurred while callers were in his office. With his face pale and twisted by pain, he continued to talk almost as if nothing were happening!

He might have survived more heart attacks but it is not likely that he could have survived the standard treatment for heart attacks in those days: boiling water poured over his chest while he lay on the floor!

At midnight on July 18, the mighty Zapotec lost his final battle.

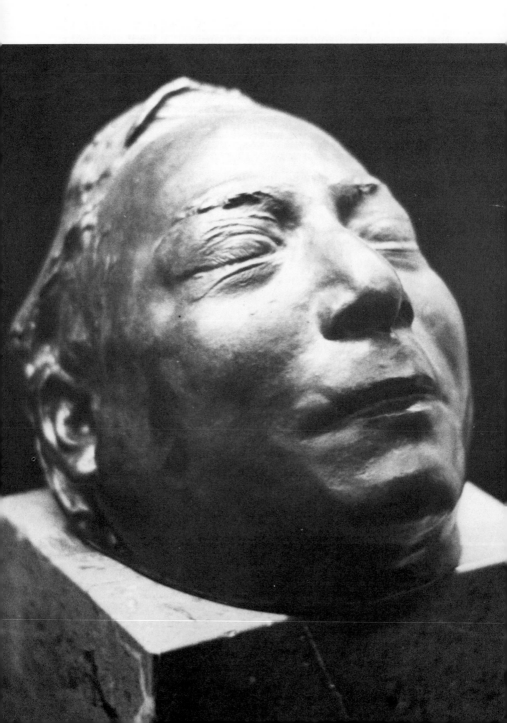

This is the death mask (a plaster cast made after death) of Benito Juárez, as displayed in the Juárez Museum in the National Palace.

In modern Mexico City, the Juárez Museum in the National Palace is a very special place of honor. (One must wipe one's shoes before entering.) Avenida Juárez is one of the city's main thoroughfares. Along it in a central gathering place, Alameda Park, is a huge, white marble monument, perhaps the most impressive in all of Mexico.

It honors the man who rode in the dusty black coach.

SEVEN
--- *The French Adventure*

FLY IN A SPIDER WEB

Suppose that, along about the time of the Civil War in the U.S., the emperor of a European country got to thinking like this:

"The U.S. is engaged in a bloody war, brother against brother. The nation is being torn apart. The U.S. form of government obviously doesn't work. Liberal democracy has broken down. They need something sensible like monarchy. They need my unemployed relative, Max, as their emperor. And Max needs the work."

"That's crazy," you say. "Couldn't happen."

Well, it didn't happen, not to the U.S. But something much like that happened to Mexico. Napoleon III of France was the emperor involved. His empress, Eugénie, also had a finger in this peculiar pie.

There were Mexicans in France in those days. Many of them were there for their health; the liberal Juárez government in Mexico made them sick to their stomachs. It happened that among these Mexicans was a handsome young fellow named José Manuel Hidalgo. The *Juaristas* had taken property from him; he had fled to Paris. Eugénie introduced Hidalgo to Napoleon. Hidalgo gave Napoleon an earful.

By the time Hidalgo and other Mexican exiles had finished, Napoleon's head was full of porridge. He developed rosy notions of a French Catholic empire stretching all the way from Texas to Panama. The ruler of this great dreamland, of course, would be a proper Catholic prince, from no less a ruling family than the Hapsburgs. You couldn't get much more royal than that.

And all of this could go on behind the back of the U.S., which would be fighting for its life in the Civil War. Napoleon thought the South might win, with a little quiet help from Europe. Then monarchy could be restored to at least that much of the upstart U.S. Ah, the dreams . . .

But what about the Mexicans in Mexico? Well, there were still many *criollos* there who wished the Spanish hadn't been kicked out in 1821. And the Catholic church was still powerful; most of the bishops and priests would welcome the French. With the help of these, surely the mighty French army could have its way against the *Juarista* mobs.

ENTER THE BUTTERFLY MAN

Meanwhile, on the sun-splashed shore of the Adriatic Sea, Austrian Archduke Maximilian and his lively duchess awoke in the castle Miramar and talked excitedly about going to Mexico. Both saw Napoleon's offer as the job opportunity of a lifetime.

The duchess, especially. Restless and ambitious, she felt that her beloved Max was being wasted. He loved to design buildings (Miramar castle was one of his designs) and to study birds and flowers and insects. Life at Miramar was pleasant, so very pleasant, but surely her husband was marked for greater things than chasing butterflies.

Napoleon made his final offer; Maximilian hesitated. He usually hesitated. Napoleon threatened to pick someone else for the glorious crown. Quickly Maximilian said, in effect, "Have no fear; I'm your boy."

"I give you," said Napoleon, "a throne on a pile of gold."

Emperor Maximilian, in all his glory. He carried a heavy load and died with dignity.

Who could resist an offer like that?

One thing especially bothered Maximilian: did the Mexican people really want him as their ruler?

Napoleon had a vote taken in Mexico. It came out the way Napoleon wanted it to come out. Yes, Mexico wanted Maximilian. (It wasn't until later that Maximilian discovered that liberals hadn't been allowed to vote.)

Napoleon had promised Maximilian that French troops would support him in Mexico until the end of 1867. In turn, Maximilian promised that the Mexican treasury would pay all the expenses of the French invasion, plus debts due to France, England and Spain, plus a batch of overdue bonds held by a money lender named Jecker.

It was understood, of course, that Max couldn't start shipping the Mexican riches right away. There would be expenses involved in setting up the new government. In other words, a pipeline would have to be built before all that silver and gold could be shipped.

French bankers sold bonds to finance the early expenses of the adventure. They were odd bonds; through one gimmick or another, two-thirds of the money remained in France. What it all amounted to was that before Maximilian even left Europe, he had managed to TRIPLE the already crushing debt of Mexico!

MIXED-UP MAX

Actually, Maximilian was a pretty decent sort of fellow. Mixed-up, but decent. He wrote to Juárez, believe it or not, and asked for his cooperation in taking over Mexico. Juárez must have been stunned. En route to Mexico, Maximilian spent most of his time writing a book of etiquette --- rules which would govern the royal court in Mexico City. (Before he finished this book, it would run to 600 pages!)

Veracruz . . . the name pops up constantly in Mexican history. Cortés and the *conquistadores* had landed near the present city site and had given it its name. The Spaniards who followed usually landed at Veracruz and left by the same water gate. The Americans landed there in 1847. Juárez, when driven out of the capital, kept his liberal government alive in Veracruz. Through Veracruz had passed much of the rich Spanish trade with the Orient.

It was liberal country, Veracruz, and nobody had asked the liberals if they wanted to live under a Hapsburg prince.

So, when the ship bearing Emperor Maximilian and Empress Carlota landed at this historic port, there was no welcoming party. There were only vultures perched on the rooftops.

They moved inland toward the capital, away from the steaming coast and the vultures. Some Indian villages offered a friendly welcome; to these natives, Maximilian was another fair-skinned, bearded Quetzalcóatl, returned from the east. Church officials were friendly, too, at first; they expected this Catholic ruler to restore church privileges and properties.

But it had to be a rude shock for Maximilian to receive this message from the headquarters of Benito Juárez at Monterrey:

"It is given a man, sir, to attack the rights of others, seize their goods, assault the lives of those who defend their nationality, make of their virtues crimes, and one's own vices a virtue, but there is one thing beyond the reach of such perversity: the tremendous judgment of history."

And in the mountains of Guerrero, the sturdy old guerrilla fighter, Juan Alvarez, issued another proclamation:

"I still live, men of the coast, I who have ever led you to fight against tyrants."

Poor Max; he had hardly set foot in the country and already he was being called a tyrant. But there was worse to come.

On their first night in Mexico City, their quarters were so full of creeping and crawling things that Maximilian, Emperor of Mexico, spent the night sleeping on a billiard table!

MAX MOVES TO THE SUBURBS

Maximilian and Carlota quickly moved out of the central city into the suburbs, to the grand old Spanish castle of Chapultepec. If there were bedbugs in this stately mansion, they at least would be of a better class.

Maximilian kept busy remodelling the castle and designing a great avenue from the castle into the heart of the city. (This

Emperor Maximilian and Empress Carlota, fresh from Europe, enter the National Palace of Mexico, unaware of waiting bedbugs. This diorama is in the Gallery of National History, Chapultepec Park, Mexico City.

avenue is now Mexico's finest --- Paseo de la Reforma.) He enjoyed making laws, even if no one paid any attention to them. Entertainment and gift-giving also delighted him. During the first six months of his rule, he gave 12 receptions, 16 balls, 20 banquets and 70 lunches. During the first year, he spent more than one hundred thousand *pesos* on wine alone! (We can probably assume that he had help in drinking it.)

To the enormous shock and disappointment of the conservatives who were depending on him, the emperor turned out to be something of a liberal. Maximilian and Carlota sometimes wore Mexican clothes and ate Mexican food. On Independence Day Maximilian went to the town of Dolores, the place of *El Grito*. There he spoke in praise of Father Hidalgo, the revolutionary, no doubt causing hundreds of his Hapsburg ancestors to spin in their graves.

Maximilian and Carlota had been told that their mission in Mexico was to protect the Catholic church from the attacks of *Juaristas*. But they soon realized that the terrible wars of the past 50 years had little to do with religion. It seemed to them that the bloodshed had to do mostly with property rights. When Maximilian refused to restore church property, many bishops and priests began to attack him.

THE SKELETON OF MEXICO

Maximilian and his wife wrote glowing letters to their relatives in Europe. Mexico was simply wonderful, they said, far ahead of Europe in almost everything.

In truth, they were shocked by the poverty and wretchedness of the people. Fifty years of internal war had stripped all meat from the bones of the country; the skeleton was a grim sight. If Napoleon really expected this helpless nation to produce great riches and be the anchor for a Latin American Catholic empire, he would have a long wait.

Yet there was a side to Mexico which fascinated Maximilian and Carlota. The colorful beauty of the landscapes was a constant source of delight. Maximilian, especially, liked to ride out of the great Valley of Mexico, over the green mountains to Cuernavaca. In this special place of tropical sunshine, Cortés had built his personal palace and José de la Borda, the silver king of Taxco, had developed lovely flower gardens. (Both can still be seen there today but now the smog of a busy, growing town makes them harder to enjoy.)

Maximilian grew ever more fond of Mexico's Indians. Their simple life close to the earth, their love of flowers and fiestas, their calm acceptance of suffering --- all warmed the emperor's heart. He began to dream of building his new empire on the sturdy base of Indian tastes and values. The *criollos* of the capital seemed much too greedy, too concerned about their own welfare, too little concerned about Mexico. The up-and-coming *mestizos* --- the mixed race --- seemed little better.

But the Indians, sitting patiently in the morning sun of a thousand little marketplaces, seemed better, cleaner, closer to the real nature of this breathtaking land. In their letters to Europe, Maximilian and Carlota began to speak of themselves as "we Mexicans."

TROUBLE BUBBLES

As time wore on, Napoleon began to have serious doubts about Maximilian's performance in Mexico. Mexican money was not flowing rapidly into the French treasury. It WAS flowing rapidly through Maximilian's extravagant fingers.

Napoleon's watchdog in Mexico City was General Bazaine. The general, with the backing of Napoleon, tightened up on the emperor of Mexico.

As 1864 neared its end, hope still remained for the grand scheme of Napoleon. The *Juaristas* still had not been conquered and continued to nip at the edges of Maximilian's empire. As poverty tightened its grip on the country, *Juaristas* by the tens of thousands asked Maximilian's government for jobs. Benito Juárez fumed and threatened to publish the list of *Juaristas* who had gone over to the enemy.

"Do that," warned one of his advisors, "and you will destroy the liberal party."

Juárez was not in a good position to argue the point. He found himself scurrying through the northern mountains, chased by General Bazaine's soldiers.

A bad year for Juárez, was 1864. But 1865 would be better and he wouldn't have to lift a finger to bring it about. Tides of

*The Borda Gardens, built in Cuernavaca by the Taxco silver king,
were a favorite resting place for Maximilian and Carlota. Today
the gardens are open to ordinary folks.*

history were moving in the world; they would soon be lapping at Mexican shores.

Early in 1865, the U.S. Civil War ended in victory for the North. Napoleon had guessed wrong again. The U.S. had no intention of allowing the French to remain in Mexico. To help get the message across, General Philip Sheridan of Civil War fame stationed his army along the Rio Grande. Piles of ammunition were left here and there, unguarded. If *Juarista* soldiers hauled off the stuff, General Sheridan didn't care too much. One had to expect losses on this wild frontier. With this kind of U.S. help, *Juarista* armies began to grow again.

Meanwhile, back in France, Napoleon noticed a lot of restless muttering around the palace. While France had been playing around in Mexico, Prussia had started to make angry noises in Europe. Napoleon realized that it was high time to bail out of the Mexican mess. He told the U.S. secretary of state, William Seward, of his sour decision.

Remember, Napoleon had promised Maximilian that French troops would protect his empire through 1867; now the ruler of France would have to back down from his word. It meant a bad smudge on the honor of Napoleon.

At least, the ruler of France decided, the world should not be able to sneer that the dirty peasants fighting under the ragged banner of Juárez had driven the proud French into the sea. He ordered Bazaine to make a final mighty effort to wipe out the *Juaristas*, then leave Mexico.

Bazaine knew that Napoleon's order could be carried out only with a quick, brutal thrust. Not the sort of thing that the butterfly-chaser cared for, at all. Bazaine, the watchdog, knew he would have to sink his teeth into the emperor's leg. He did.

"DEATH TO THE BANDITS!"

Bazaine's first move was to force Maximilian to issue a harsh decree: anyone caught fighting the French would be shot. The angry slogan of the French became "Death to the Bandits!"

It is said that Maximilian signed the decree only after being told that Juárez had left the country; this was a lie.

One of the first *Juaristas* to pay with his life was a highly respected general named Arteaga. But, after some early success with his cruel campaign, Bazaine began to slip.

In the south, the *mestizo* general, Porfirio Díaz, was organizing guerrillas for a march on the capital. *Juarista* troops, aided by U.S. supplies, were roaming the country, striking hard with hit-and-run attacks.

Poor Maximilian . . . his world of sunshine and flowers was turning to ashes before his eyes. He found it hard to believe that Napoleon would actually break his word. Again and again he sent messengers to the French ruler, pleading that he change his mind, insisting that there was still hope for their Mexican adventure.

At last a desperate Carlota left for Europe to argue the case with Napoleon, and even with the Pope in Rome, if he could be approached. But poor Carlota's mind had snapped under the strain of the Mexico years; she could not make her case in Europe. It may have been too late, anyway.

Napoleon had always planned that at the proper moment, Maximilian would give up his throne and sail back to Europe, working on his manual of court etiquette along the way. Maximilian may have thought this, too, on Monday, but by Tuesday, he had changed his mind. He would stay in Mexico. By the next Monday, he had changed his mind again.

When he heard that Carlota had gone out of her mind, he wanted to leave Mexico to be with her. He even wrote a proclamation of abdication and ordered his baggage shipped to Veracruz. But Maximilian went only as far as Orizaba, where he spent six weeks studying butterflies and changing his mind.

At the end of November, Maximilian had decided to remain in Mexico. It was a grand gesture, but as it turned out, it was a very foolish one.

THE LAST ACT

General Bazaine made one last attempt to persuade Maximilian to leave. When the emperor refused, Bazaine decided that it was time to take his soldiers and run.

168

Maximilian had this notion --- Bazaine thought it was silly --- that he could still defeat the *Juaristas*; after all, there would remain a Mexican conservative army of at least 15,000 men. So Bazaine threw cold water on this idea by destroying all surplus cannon and ammunition.

But still Maximilian refused to leave.

The conservative generals Miramón and Mejía were set up at Querétaro, north of the capital. Another conservative army held Puebla. *Juaristas* in large numbers were moving toward Querétaro, while Díaz was pushing an army up from the south, itching for a fight with the conservatives at Puebla.

On February 13, 1867, Emperor Maximilian rode toward Querétaro to take personal command of his army. Eight or nine thousand against 40,000 --- those were the odds against Maximilian. A born loser would have loved the situation. The town, in a valley surrounded by low hills, would be hard to defend; in fact, it was a trap.

"Attack," Miramón advised Maximilian, attack before the *Juaristas* have gathered all their forces for the big blow. "Wait," advised Márquez, wait until the *Juaristas* have crowded in, then attack and destroy them all with one blow.

Maximilian, no military genius, chose to wait.

The *Juaristas* cut off food supply to the town on March 6.

Maximilian, the Hapsburg prince, lived like a common soldier, sleeping on the ground. He exposed himself to the enemy guns again and again, winning the admiration of his soldiers. It seems likely that he wanted to die in battle. Such an end appealed to his romantic soul, to his idea of what was right and proper for a Hapsburg prince.

Chapultepec Castle, perched on a high hill, was built by Spanish rulers, then rebuilt by almost every one who has lived in it. Originally it was in the suburbs; now the city surrounds it. The last rebuilding turned the great stone pile into a fine history museum. Maximilian loved the monstrous place, as you can imagine, and laid out a great boulevard, Paseo de la Reforma, from the castle to downtown Mexico City, so that he could go to the office in style every morning. The airplane? Around the turn of the century, when this picture was taken, photographers loved to take pictures of airplanes.

So calm was Maximilian, it was said, that during dull moments in the fighting, he put on his glasses and worked on his manual of court etiquette!

By mid-May, the end was near. Betrayed once by Napoleon, Maximilian was about to be betrayed again, this time by a Mexican. A desperate plan had been agreed upon. At midnight of May 14, Maximilian's forces would launch an all-out attack. If they could fight their way clear of the town, they would join the Indian tribesmen of General Mejïa.

Chances of success were slim. Still, the plan promised the kind of dramatic end that Maximilian longed for. If he had to go, he wanted to go with a bang, leading his loyal troops as a Hapsburg was born to do.

Among his forces was a young Mexican officer, Miguel López. A charming fellow, but tricky, López had no interest in dying so young in a doomed cause.

So López made a deal with the *Juaristas*. He would let the enemy into town before the planned breakout. In return, he wanted money for himself and a promise that Maximilian could go free. A *Juarista* leader named Escobeda agreed. But first Maximilian had to be talked into delaying the attack; this was done.

At three a.m., Miguel López allowed the *Juaristas* to steal through the gloom into town at the point in the fortifications where he was in command. Quickly, Querétaro fell. The last battle in Maximilian's tragic war had ended in treachery.

But Maximilian refused to run, despite the urging of López. Instead he went to the Hill of the Bells at the edge of town to join Mejïa in surrender. It was a splendid moment for the emperor, but it must have been a bitter one, too.

Bells rang through the town at dawn. They were victory bells for the liberals. For Maximilian, they were the bells of death.

Benito Juárez had won the victory at last. There could be no question in his mind about proper punishment for Maximilian. European nations must be put on notice forever that Mexico belonged to Mexicans.

As Maximilian waited in jail, the royal families of Europe pleaded with Juárez to show mercy. Friends of Juárez in the U.S. added their pleas. The Indian was unmoved. Too many of his followers had died. "Death to the Bandits" was a two-edged sword and now, at long last, the sword was in his hands.

In prison, as the end neared, more escape plots blossomed. One of Maximilian's officers, a German prince named Salm, arranged one that might have worked. With help from his wife, Salm bribed the prison guards.

But Maximilian wanted to know: could Miramón and Mejía escape with him?

"No," said Salm.

"No," said Maximilian. He would have no part of the plan unless his loyal generals could go, too.

There was another part of the plan which he didn't care for at all. The Salms wanted him to disguise himself by shaving his beard.

But suppose he were recaptured without his beard, asked Maximilian; what would happen to the Hapsburg dignity then?

On June 19, Maximilian died before a firing squad on the Hill of the Bells. His loyal generals, Miramón and Mejía, died with him.

Today, on the Hill of the Bells, a monument supplied by the French honors Maximilian. Mexicans could not let it stand alone. Their monument at the same site honors Benito Juárez. There is something very right about these two enemies being together on this historic hill.

The French adventure in Mexico was probably doomed from the beginning. It might now be little more than a minor paragraph in Mexican history if Napoleon hadn't chosen this peculiar man, Maximilian, to represent him. The man who studied insects turned out to be just a fly in a spider web . . . but a special kind of fly.

Actually, Max was a pretty decent sort of fellow, for an emperor.

An artist shows the execution of Maximilian, at right, and generals Miramón and Mejía on the Hill of the Bells, Querétaro.

EIGHT
--- The Díaz Dictatorship

"A DOG WITH A BONE
IN ITS MOUTH..."

When the black carriage of Benito Juárez entered Mexico City in July, 1867, it was met by a young general who hoped to ride with the new president to the National Palace.

The general had fought well in the liberal ranks; he had Indian blood; he came from the home town of Juárez. Juárez had been his teacher in Oaxaca. The general had even spent 20,000 *pesos* of his own money to decorate the streets for this great day. It seemed only fitting that now, in this moment of triumph, he should be allowed to join the president.

But the general, Porfirio Díaz, was not asked to ride with Juárez. Instead, he was passed by with a cold nod.

Perhaps Juárez was thinking that he would soon have to cut off from the government payroll thousands of the soldiers who had fought in his cause. To share this glorious day with a general of that army might have seemed improper. What matters is that on that day, Juárez turned a strong supporter into a bitter enemy. He may also have created the monster whose cold steel hand would hold Mexico in its grip for 30 years.

Porfirio Díaz ran for president against Juárez only a few months after the snub. There was only one other candidate, Sebastián Lerdo de Tejada. Díaz finished a poor third. He retired to his farm in Oaxaca to grow sugar cane. After all, he was young; he could wait.

Then, in 1872, Juárez died and Lerdo became president. In special elections held that fall, Lerdo was re-elected easily. Back to Oaxaca went Porfirio Díaz.

By 1876, Díaz had grown tired of waiting. When Lerdo announced that he would run again, Díaz issued the Plan of Tuxtepec; it was the customary way of telling Mexicans that revolution was brewing. (Interesting thing about the Plan of Tuxtepec --- one of its provisions was that a president could serve for only one term, with no re-election. The day would come when Díaz wished he had said something else.)

Díaz went north to talk to important *gringos*. U.S. officials gave him money and other encouragement. In disguise, Díaz sneaked back into the country via Veracruz, then went to Oaxaca and gathered up some of his old soldiers. On to Mexico City!

At Tecoac on November 16, 1876, the Díaz army defeated the Lerdo army. Lerdo ran off to New York City. Díaz strolled into the capital and said, in effect, "Mexicans, I am your new president."

A few months later, Congress made it official. At age 46, Porfirio Díaz became president of Mexico. He would be president of Mexico for 30 out of the 39 years of life left to him.

But, you say, what of the Plan of Tuxtepec, which called for a one-term presidency? Well, times change and one must bend with the winds. Díaz came up with that idea, remember, when somebody else was president.

JUMP OR BE SHOT

Porfirio Díaz liked the life of a soldier. The discipline, the action, the no-nonsense part of it --- these appealed strongly to him. An officer ordered and a soldier jumped . . . or was shot; it seemed like a sensible way to live . . . or die. He demonstrated early in life, though, that he much preferred to be the one who

*The Man himself, Don Porfirio Díaz, ablaze with gilt and medals.
He tried to look the part of caudillo, or military dictator.*

ordered, not the one who jumped. The one who lived, not the one who died.

No one ever questioned his courage. It was Porfirio Díaz who had set up the fortifications of Puebla against the French invasion; the great *Cinco de Mayo* victory belonged to him as much as to anyone.

The French caught him in Oaxaca, though, and jailed him in a convent. For five months, Díaz patiently dug an escape tunnel. Then, when the tunnel was nearly finished, the French transferred him to another convent!

No tunnels this time. A little bribery got him some rope and a knife. Come one very dark night, Díaz listened for the steps of the guard in the courtyard below his cell, then, at the right moment, climbed onto the window sill and flung a rope. Missed. Again. Missed. Again . . .

When the rope finally looped around a chimney, he pulled himself over the roof, across the slippery tiles, away from the courtyard. Hanging from the rope, he lowered himself toward the ground outside the convent wall.

The gloom of the night could hide many dangers; it could hide a pig, even. The pig wasn't a problem until Díaz's knife slipped out of his belt and landed point first. On the pig. The pig, of course, ripped open the darkness with a terrified squeal, bringing the guard clattering across the cobblestones.

Díaz, the man of patience, dangled in the darkness from the rope for what must have seemed like hours.

At last, the guard went back to the courtyard. Díaz cautiously slipped down, waited a moment in the mud of the pig-pen, then dashed to freedom. Before long, his guerrilla army was pestering the French again.

In 1876, without really knowing what it was getting into, Mexico had elected as its president a brown-skinned tiger who would make even Santa Anna look like a pussycat.

"Bread or the Club" --- this soon became the slogan of the Díaz administration.

Meaning? Just this: if you went along with the administration, good things came your way. If you protested or resisted, you got your skull cracked.

There was plenty of bread to pass out. Land, government jobs, mineral rights --- whatever Díaz controlled, which was practically everything, he gave away or sold to those who would support his government. He did not seem to be interested in riches for himself. He wanted power and he found that he could buy it.

"A dog with a bone in its mouth," Díaz once remarked, "neither kills nor steals."

So he passed out rewards to his enemies as well as to his friends. He knew that many of his enemies wanted power only as a steppingstone to riches. If they could have riches without power, they would let Díaz have the power. So Díaz fed their greed . . . and kept his power.

The government of Benito Juaréz had aimed for freedom with progress. The Díaz government was willing to pass up freedom in exchange for what it called progress. There were railroads to be built, oil wells to be drilled, farms to be developed.

Díaz knew he would need help from outside Mexico. Word was passed that foreigners were welcome again. U.S. and European companies quickly got the message. Díaz gave them great chunks of government land and asked little in return but development. More land was taken from the hungry Indians and handed over to the foreign robber barons.

Before foreigners would feel safe in Mexico, though, the countryside had to be tamed. Díaz knew exactly how to do it. First, the battling politicians who had torn Mexico apart for 50 years had to be simmered down; they all got a bone to chew on, courtesy of Díaz. But there was another problem . . .

BANDIDOS!

Remember those thousands of soldiers who had been fired by Juárez? Many of them had turned to banditry; no trail in Mexico was safe from them. Díaz knew that something would have to be done about the terrible *bandidos* before Mexico could be considered under his control.

So he set up a roving police force called *rurales*. He gave them weapons and horses, then decked them out in gray uniforms with silver buttons. Dashing red scarves and broadbrimmed hats topped off the costume. *Rurales* were ordered to shoot

A unit of rurales, feared throughout the land during the Díaz regime, lines up for inspection.

lawbreakers on sight; there would be no judges, no trials, no sentences. In short order, roaming *rurales* brought a kind of peace and quiet to the countryside that hadn't been known since the days of Spanish rule. *Bandidos* mostly disappeared; it was like a miracle.

But the *bandidos* hadn't disappeared at all; they had merely put on gray uniforms! The sly Díaz didn't mind bandits and murderers so long as they were HIS bandits and murderers. So, over the length and breadth of Mexico, wherever *rurales* rode, fear rode with them.

Small wonder. Listen to this terrible story:

There were some brave Indians in the state of Hidalgo who loved their land. When the government told them they must give it up, they refused. The *rurales* were called. The brave Indians were captured, then buried up to their necks in the land they loved. The *rurales*, whooping and hollering, galloped their horses over them, again and again . . .

There was a law which made the work of the *rurales* much easier. *"Ley Fuga,"* it was called, or "Law of Flight." Under *Ley Fuga*, a policeman could legally shoot a prisoner who was trying to escape. Naturally, if a *rural* said his prisoner was trying to escape, and the prisoner was dead, who could say the *rural* was lying? *Ley Fuga* must have come in handy for the *rurales*, because the law was used as an excuse for killing more than 10,000 persons during the Díaz dictatorship!

THE PUPPET GONZALEZ

Remember the Plan of Tuxtepec, which Díaz had put forth before he became president? It called for a one-term presidency. The first term of Porfirio Díaz ended in 1880.

Díaz didn't hanker to go back to growing sugar cane in Oaxaca. He just plain liked the job of president. And hadn't Mexico made wonderful progress during his first four years? The civil wars had ended, the roads were safe again and the rich were getting richer.

As the end of his term neared, Díaz apparently didn't feel strong enough to say, "I didn't really mean it, folks," about the Plan of Tuxtepec. He did feel strong enough, though, to pick a

Late in the reign of Díaz, as the old man's grip weakened, news-paper cartoonists began to take pot shots at him. Here he gives in-structions to a political puppet.

personal friend to fill in --- General Manuel González, an old buddy from the soldiering days.

There is a question about the record of González as president of Mexico. Was he the worst president Mexico had ever had? Or was he just one of the worst? González made himself and his friends rich. He gave away even more of Mexico to foreigners than Díaz had. The peasants got even less under González than they had under Díaz.

While González was cleaning out the cupboard, what of Díaz? He was able to keep himself amused. He got married, for one thing. In 1881, at age 51, he married a 16-year-old girl, Carmen Rubio. (His first wife had died much earlier.) In 1882, he was appointed to the Supreme Court and the Senate. He quit both of these jobs to become governor of Oaxaca. Then, in 1883, he travelled to the U.S., where the robber barons welcomed him as one of their own. While González was a fine fellow, they said, he couldn't last; they could hardly wait until Porfirio Díaz would be president of Mexico again.

They didn't have long to wait. Díaz was elected in 1884. For the next 26 years, the steel-hard *mestizo* would clamp his grip on suffering Mexico.

An incredible thing happened in Mexico in 1894. The budget was balanced! After decades of running into debt to its knees, then to its waist, then up to its neck, Mexico was actually taking in as much money as it was paying out! The miracle was properly celebrated. Díaz got most of the credit but actually, credit should have gone to José Limantour, his very clever minister of finance.

Minerals from the mines of Mexico flowed north to the U.S. on railroads built by *gringos*. Industry in the U.S., growing at a rapid rate, was hungry for the silver, gold, copper, lead and zinc of Mexico. Díaz was quite willing to let the U.S. have it. Europe was an eager market for the bananas, sugar, coffee and henequen (also called sisal) produced on Mexico's fertile land under Mexico's endless sun. Díaz saw to it that Europe got what it wanted.

One thing Díaz did was build railroads, no easy job in Mexico's mountains. Wild sights like this were common as trains emerged from hundreds of tunnels.

WHERE DID ALL THE LIBERALS GO?

How was Porfirio Díaz able to grip and hold Mexico for so long? What happened to the Constitution of 1857? Had the liberal ideas of Benito Juárez been forgotten so soon?

The Díaz dictatorship seems a little hard to explain unless one remembers these facts: after the Spanish were kicked out of the country, Mexico wasn't really governed for more than 40 years. Yes, there was a president in the National Palace most of the time; there were bureaucrats, of course; there was an army of sorts. But often the government dangled at the end of a thin rope; the first strong revolutionary breeze or extra drain on the treasury would send it crashing to the ground.

Then the French, under Napoleon III, went out of their minds for a moment and invaded Mexico. Miracle of miracles! The Mexicans stopped fighting among themselves and united under Juárez to throw back the invader. On *Cinco de Mayo*, the haughty French were whipped at Puebla. General Bazaine and Maximilian had "Death to the Bandits!" thrown back into their teeth at Querétaro. Mexico for the Mexicans! The whole country could rally behind an idea like that.

And did. When Juárez took over the capital for the last time in 1867, he had the support of a united Mexico, at long last. When re-elected in 1871, he had started Mexico down the road to progress with freedom. But in 1872, he died; Mexico was not quite ready to live without him.

It is quite possible that if Benito Juárez had lived through three more years as president, Mexico would have gained 50 years in its staggering advance toward justice for all. If Juárez had lived, there might have been no Díaz dictatorship. If there had been no Díaz dictatorship, Mexico might have avoided the terrible mess which came after.

The tragedy of Mexico in the last century might be stated simply --- Benito Juárez died too soon.

If you lived in Mexico during the Díaz dictatorship --- in the right neighborhood and in the right income bracket --- you might very well ask, "Who's complaining?"

If you were an Indian living in the wrong neighborhood, you might very well ask, "Who isn't? Except those of us ridden down by *rurales* . . ."

What happened to Mexico during the Díaz years is almost beyond belief.

Díaz referred to the Congress as *"mi caballada,"* or "my herd of tame horses." Elections were a joke. Díaz picked the winning candidates. Occasionally a mistake was made; more than once, the list of candidates for office carried the name of a person who wasn't even alive! *No importe;* Díaz could hardly be expected to keep tabs on the health of all his friends.

Naturally, voters stopped going to the polls. It was difficult for the government to keep up the appearance of honest elections. The situation became so serious that in one state, prisoners in the penitentiary were put to work. They filled out enough ballots to stuff the boxes!

Listen to this: during a period of 11 years, Porfirio Díaz turned over ONE-FIFTH of Mexico's land to friends and real estate promoters! At the close of the Díaz dictatorship, less than ten per cent of the Indian population of Mexico had any land at all.

Thirty million acres of Baja California were passed along to just four persons. In the state of Chihuahua, a single person got 17 million acres.

Toward the end of the Díaz dictatorship, almost all of the wealth of Mexico was held by a mere three per cent of the population. And most of that wealth was in the hands of foreigners, not Mexicans. The sad slogan became: "Mexico --- mother of foreigners, stepmother of Mexicans."

What happened to the peasant population? Mostly, they went hungry. Díaz not only sold and gave away land, he also handed out water rights. Peasant lands turned to dust.

Listen to this, too: in the last years of the Díaz dictatorship, three-fourths of the Mexican population was composed of farmers. Yet Mexico, in those years, could not feed itself! It was necessary to import food.

Progress?

Avenida Juárez intersects with Paseo de la Reforma in Mexico City. This photograph probably was made about 1920. In background at left is the skeleton of the new National Palace begun by Porfirio Díaz. Now it is the Monument to the Revolution. This intersection today is a nightmare of traffic, smog and noise.

Benito Juárez would have called it something else.

The Díaz regime ended in 1910. The end came as a surprise to the fat cats. They had come to believe that somehow Porfirio Díaz would be Big Daddy forever.

But the pressures had been building, just as steam builds in a boiler. An old boiler becomes rusty around its seams. Porfirio Díaz was nearing his 80th year of life; his seams were rusting, too.

Prosperity was slipping away in 1908. Mexico had become dependent on the health of foreign business; in 1907, Wall Street, U.S.A., had come down with a bad case of the croup.

Díaz probably saw the end approaching. An American newspaperman named Creelman had talked himself into an interview with the Mexican leader. Díaz told Creelman that he had become a dictator only to make Mexico safe for democracy. He said also that he would retire in 1910.

Díaz retiring? Porfirio Díaz? The blockbuster interview was published first in the U.S. Mexican publications picked it up quickly, of course. The grapevine began to hum: Díaz may not be forever, after all. Quietly, just a whisper: *Viva Revolución!*

What is barely believable is that the almighty dictatorship of Porfirio Díaz, *caudillo* to end all *caudillos*, was about to be smashed to the ground by a five-foot, two-inch vegetarian with a squeaky voice.

Really. It happened in Mexico in 1910.

Every November 20, Mexico celebrates the end of the rule of Porfirio Díaz with a great parade. Seventy thousand persons took part in this one; millions more watched. The parade ended at the Revolution Monument in the background, which was begun by Díaz as a new National Palace, then left unfinished. An ugly monument to an ugly man...

NINE

--- Díaz, Madero and Death

THE MEXICAN MAXIMILIAN

Take a soft-spoken little man who believes in spirits and a vegetable diet. Give him a genteel upbringing in a rich family. Then have him write a polite little book.

Believe it or not, you have just created a recipe for bloody revolution.

The man was Francisco Madero. Like Maximilian, he was well-educated. His wealthy family had been able to send him to schools in Europe and to the University of California in Berkeley. Like Maximilian, he had liberal ideas about government which were not those of the rich, powerful persons around him. Like Maximilian, he trusted his family and friends too much. Like Maximilian, he failed.

The Madero family was *criollo*; their fortune had come from trading, ranching and mining. The Madero family thought Francisco was strange. And not just because he believed in spirits, either.

Put in charge of a family plantation, he did a good job, up to a point. He earned profits, as a good manager should. Then

This print from a lantern slide, probably taken near Ciudad Juárez, shows Francisco Madero talking things over with an aide.

he took the profits and spent them on houses and schools and the like for the peons who worked on the land. He had this peculiar notion that if you treat people better, they work better. There was even a vicious rumor circulated that he fed as many as 100 of the children in his own home every day.

It is probably not surprising that such a man would be disturbed by the murders committed under the Díaz dictatorship. Being the kind of person he was, though, Francisco Madero did not grab a rifle and march on the capital. Instead, he wrote a book. It was a sneaky little book called "The Presidential Succession of 1910." Madero did not say, "Díaz must go." He said, in effect, "Díaz will stay but the people ought to elect the vice-president." Pretty mild stuff.

Madero began to give speeches in his high-pitched voice. He began to draw crowds. He started a newspaper and organized what were called anti-reelection clubs. In April, 1910, Madero's group managed to hold a convention. Madero, of course, was nominated to run for president.

The dictator began to take notice. Nothing for Díaz to worry about, of course; such a pipsqueak couldn't possibly stir up any real trouble. But to be on the safe side, Díaz asked Madero to drop by the National Palace for a little chat. Madero was happy to oblige.

What Madero really had in mind, said the little man in his squeaky voice, was to try to get Mexicans to take voting seriously; nothing more.

Díaz, of course, thought that was a fine idea. He had always believed in elections, as long as they were neat, orderly and came out right.

After the meeting with Madero, Díaz felt better. How could such an impractical person be a threat to the mighty Porfirio Díaz?

Francisco Madero was about to show him how.

ENOUGH IS ENOUGH

Crowds grew at the Madero meetings. No matter where the little man went, he found enthusiasm for his cause. Maybe the feeling was more anti-Díaz than pro-Madero but it didn't matter.

Dead Mexicans litter the street in front of the National Palace, Mexico City. Since the power was here, this place was the scene of much fighting ... and dying.

Mexico was stirring; the natives were getting very restless. The turning point for Díaz came in May, when 30,000 Madero followers demonstrated in the great plaza before the National Palace.

Enough, muttered Díaz, is enough; he clapped Madero into jail in San Luis Potosí. The charge: plotting revolution. This was in June, 1910, with the election only a month away.

Madero didn't just sulk in his lonely cell; he wrote his Plan of San Luis Potosí, under which his revolution would go forward.

Porfirio Díaz planned a great year for himself. His 80th birthday was nearing. Also, on September 16, a huge celebration would mark the moment of El Grito de Dolores 100 years earlier, when Father Hidalgo launched the revolt against Spain. There would be great parades and banquets, pageants and balls. Important persons from around the world would be on hand to honor Mexico. And, of course, to honor Porfirio Díaz, who was eager to take credit for everything good that had happened.

Not everybody got into the spirit of the occasion, however. On September 11, mounted policemen had to trample Madero followers who were making a fuss on the Paseo de la Reforma. They had even thrown rocks through the windows of the home of President Díaz! Outrageous!

(Come to think about it, though, maybe those rock throwers HAD gotten into the spirit of the occasion. Father Hidalgo didn't start his historic uproar just to turn the country over to a tyrant like Porfirio Díaz. Had Mexico broken its Spanish chains only to wear homemade ones? Maybe the person of Madero didn't matter; maybe he just happened to be at the right place waving the right banner at the right time. History is like that.)

With the big centennial celebration out of the way, Díaz announced the election results. Guess what? Díaz won. Madero got 196 votes. Another candidate got 187. (One wonders who was in charge of dreaming up the numbers.)

With Díaz safely in office for another six years, Francisco Madero was released on bail. He quickly crossed the border to San Antonio. There he published his Plan of San Luis Potosí.

The election was null and void, cried Madero. Then he proclaimed himself provisional president of Mexico and called for a national uprising on November 20.

Friends in the state of Coahuila said they would supply an army. Some army! Madero crossed the border into his homeland and promptly got lost. But at last he made contact with his "army" --- 25 men, only half of them armed.

Madero returned to Texas. This, believe it or not, was the beginning of a revolution which succeeded. A strange land, Mexico, a place of miracles. Is it not true?

ZAPATA, VILLA AND SMOKE

The seed planted by Madero was sprouting wildly in the fertile ground of Mexico. In the north, a *bandido* named Pancho Villa had begun to steal from the right people and thus became a hero to the peons. In the highlands of Morelos, a lean, dark Indian named Emiliano Zapata had formed an army. Clad in the peon uniform of white cotton, Zapata's troops made nothing but trouble for *hacendados*, the landowners.

Touched off by these firebrands, revolutionary smoke began to rise around the country. Riding the smoke cloud was the gentle little man, Francisco Madero.

It didn't take long to topple Díaz, once the movement got underway. The dictator had grown old in office. He was no longer the powerful soldier who had roared north out of Oaxaca. His government had grown old, too; his state governors were mostly men living out their last years in splendid ease. To make matters worse for the dictatorship, the army had been allowed to wither. On paper, Díaz could call on 30,000 soldiers; in fact, there were only 18,000. Most of these were poorly armed; the long years of graft in government purchasing had sucked the army's blood.

José Limantour, the dictator's righthand man, had been in Europe. When he returned, he talked first not to Díaz, his boss, but to the Madero forces. Anything but a fool, Limantour wanted to keep himself and his friends in power. He was prepared to dump even the great dictator himself to bring this about.

In the north, the hard-riding armies of Pancho Villa and Pascual Orozco won battle after battle. In the south, Emiliano

A common scene in Mexico during the bloody years. These Villistas were hanged near Chihuahua by order of a Federal general. They probably hung there a good long while.

In this cozy scene, Francisco Madero, provisional president of Mexico, reads what must be a letter of congratulations. His wife stands directly behind him in this 1911 photo. One wonders about the rag tied over the trigger of the rifle in the foreground.

Zapata and his peons swept aside the federal soldiers and captured Cuatla on May 12.

(Some Americans were so eager to help Villa that they were willing even to steal for him. In El Paso, Texas, the Pioneer Club had mounted an old cannon in a park. Four or five Texans decided the weapon might be useful in Mexico, so one dark night they stole it, hid it for a while, then smuggled it across the border buried in a wagon under hay and household effects. There is some doubt about how useful the cannon was to Madero forces but at least the terrible roar apparently frightened the enemy a few times. After Madero's victory, the governor of the state of Chihuahua ordered the weapon returned to El Paso. Amid great ceremony and speechmaking, the cannon was hooked to a car and hauled across the bridge connecting Ciudad Juarez and El Paso. At last report, the cannon was still in El Paso . . . unless someone has stolen it.)

Once back in Mexico City, Limantour tried to get a grip on a government that was slipping away like a greased pig. He failed.

THE HEADLIGHT TREATY

The agreement which ended the revolt was signed near Ciudad Juárez on May 21, at 10:30 p.m. A historic first: automobile headlights provided light for the signing on a table set up outside of town.

Under the agreement, Díaz and Limantour would resign. A temporary president would be appointed to serve until elections in October, 1911. It was taken for granted that Francisco Madero would be the choice of the people.

On May 23, the announcement was made in Mexico City. On the next day, the halls of government filled with mobs crying out against the dictator, "Resign! Resign!" Even the herd of tame horses, the caballada in the Congress, passed a resolution asking for resignation.

Díaz, at home on the Calle Cadena, wasn't yet ready to quit. His friends and relatives gathered around his bed and urged him to resign. Why was Díaz in bed? As if all his other troubles weren't enough, the poor man had a terrible toothache!

It was enough to make even a caudillo cry.

Madero soldiers are caught by a brave or foolish photographer as they charge the barracks defended by Díaz troops at Ciudad Juárez.

206

THE BLOODY TIME

There had to be a tragedy. The brutal regime of Porfirio Díaz could not slide into the dustbin of history so easily, so quietly, with so little bloodshed.

The federal soldiers were stationed on the roof of the National Palace east of the plaza and in towers of the huge cathedral north of the plaza. As the great crowd gathered to roar against Díaz, someone ordered "Fire!" Guns ripped at the crowd from the heights, from the church and from the seat of their government. More than 200 died.

Even this bloodbath did not clear the plaza. It began to rain, finally. At last the mob slipped away, leaving only the dead behind.

Díaz did not resign until after midnight. Through the night, the capital vibrated to the sounds of citizens beating on tin cans, shouting, singing, dancing.

Early on the morning of May 26, Porfirio Díaz went to the San Lazaro railroad station and boarded a train to Veracruz. At Veracruz, he took passage for Europe. The dictator would not see his homeland again.

For Porfirio Díaz, it had to be a sad journey, even without a toothache. For Francisco Madero, it was the best journey of his life. Díaz was being thrown out of Mexico; Madero was being taken to its heart as few Mexican leaders ever have been.

Bienvenido, Madero!

Along the rail line from the north, crowds gathered to cheer their little hero, the destroyer of Díaz, the idol of the common people. They threw flowers; they waved flags. At San Pedro de las Colonias, his old home town, girls sang the Mexican national anthem. This went on for four days and four nights. Mexican trains have a habit of not running on time but this was ridiculous. Under normal conditions on this route, the train reached Mexico City in 30 hours! As the train crawled southward, citizens walked and rose burros and horses to the rail line to cheer, *"Viva Madero! Viva Madero!"*

In the golden sunshine of that moment, it was easy to believe that great days lay ahead.

He arrived at the capital in the middle of the morning, June 7, 1911. Shortly before dawn on that day, a remarkable event took place --- an earthquake gave the city a good hard shake. As many as a quarter of a million persons had slept in the parks and in the streets that night; they had come from outside the city to witness the great arrival. The church of Santo Domingo was ruined; an army barracks collapsed, killing 33 soldiers. The final death toll in the city was 207.

But the most interesting damage was a great crack which appeared in the National Palace. It moved the keystone of the arch under which Porfirio Díaz had passed during his long years of power.

"See?" muttered superstitious Díaz supporters. "God is angry at what Madero has done."

Madero supporters disagreed. It was a good sign, surely. The earth trembles at the arrival of Madero --- *fantástico!*

Despite the earthquake, the streets of Mexico echoed with happiness on June 7. Madero had come; Díaz had gone; now life would be sweet.

It was a fiesta, the best of fiestas. But, like all fiestas, it had to end. Everyone woke up on the morning after in the real world.

In the Mexico of 1911, what was the real world? With all the cheering and flagwaving, there was still a government to run. In October, there was an election, as promised. What's more, it was an honest election, which surprised practically everybody. And Madero was the choice of practically everybody, which surprised nobody. A newspaperman from Yucatán, Pino Suárez, was elected vice-president.

Madero took office on November 6. Mexicans sat back to watch the expected miracles.

But they didn't come. Francisco Madero, as it turned out, didn't really understand what the people wanted from him.

Land reform? It had been mentioned in the Plan of San Luis Potosí but Madero didn't seem to take it seriously. The Indians whose land had been stolen took it seriously; they expected Madero to get it back for them. When the president made no quick moves in this direction, the grumbling began.

The people, Madero said in a speech, were crying out for political freedom, not bread. Well, they wanted both, of course, but if they had to choose between them, they would choose bread. Madero did not understand this. The little man from the north saw his revolution as a revolt against Díaz, the man. The people saw it as a chance to get rid of not only Díaz but also of his whole corrupt clan. And while they were tinkering with the system, they also wanted to eliminate *criollo* landowners and throw out the foreigners who were sucking Mexico's lifeblood away.

Madero believed in free, honest elections, in real democracy for Mexico. He did not see that in a country where three-fourths of the population were unable to read or write, democracy could not work.

Francisco Madero felt brotherly love for everyone he dealt with. He always took it for granted that everyone was as honest and as dedicated as himself. As it turned out, he should not have trusted even the members of his own family.

Madero's brother, Gustavo, quickly became the strong man of the government. He organized a group of hoodlums to go around browbeating political enemies, Díaz-style. Other family members moved into the capital and began to operate as if they owned the place.

Madero had been in office less than a year when important supporters began to drift away. Emiliano Zapata, who had always had his doubts about the little man, went back to Morelos. Soon the looting and burning resumed. Pascual Orozco was next to "pronounce" against Madero --- that is, tell the world that he no longer believed in the government and wanted to bring it down.

With the pressure building, a nervous Madero made serious mistakes. To chase Orozco out of the country, he chose a general who would turn out to be one of the truly great monsters of Mexican history --- Victoriano Huerta. Huerta was well on the way to drinking himself to death; he was also a clever general who got things done.

Then Madero did something that shook the foundations of the Mexican military system. Huerta had been given a million

The dead and wounded fell in battle after battle, until Mexico was bathed in blood...again. This young rebel was photographed about 1912.

pesos to finance his campaign against Orozco. When Huerta returned to the capital after driving his victim into exile, Madero asked the general to account for the spending of the money! (Madero may not have realized that one simply didn't do this to a Mexican general.)

Stunned, outraged and insulted, Huerta refused. Madero had no choice but to retire the general. Leaving an angry Huerta with nothing to do but drink and brood would turn out to be a ghastly mistake.

Soon two other generals, Bernardo Reyes and Félix Díaz (nephew of the great Porfirio) pronounced against Madero. Clearly, the government was coming unglued.

DEATH IN THE MORNING

On a Sunday morning in early February, General Reyes led troops in a march on the National Palace. Reyes had been led to believe that the palace guard would lay down its arms. But Gustavo Madero, hearing of the uprising, had rushed to the National Palace and talked the soldiers on guard into remaining loyal.

So when the Reyes forces attacked, they were blasted by machine guns. Reyes was killed, along with several hundred innocent persons who were on their way to mass at the cathedral. Again the great plaza, scene of many historic bloodbaths, was littered with bodies.

But compared to what was coming, this was only a small tragedy. Frightened and suspicious of most of his generals, President Madero then did an amazing thing. To command the defense of the National Palace, he called on none other than the drunken monster, Victoriano Huerta!

Now the stage was set for one of the most disgraceful episodes of Mexican history, the "Tragic Ten Days."

About one and one-half kilometers away from the National Palace in Mexico City is the *Ciudadela*, an old fortress with walls more than one meter thick. Between the *Ciudadela* and the palace is the main business district of the city. This crowded area was to be the battleground. General Félix Díaz had holed up at the *Ciudadela;* General Huerta commanded at the palace.

It was a fake war; only the blood was real.

How fake? General Huerta wanted to bring down the Madero government just as badly as Díaz did, that's how fake. But Huerta wanted to follow Madero as president, so he had to make it look good.

The cannonading went on for ten days. The business district of the city was battered with shells and bullets; civilians by the hundreds were killed or maimed. When Huerta "attacked" the *Ciudadela*, he sent army units known to be loyal to Madero. They were ordered to attack without cover; they were slaughtered, as Huerta knew they would be.

The bodies of the dead, mostly innocent civilians, were scattered about the streets in such numbers that they were a traffic hazard. It was impossible to give so many a decent burial, so the bodies were splashed with kerosene and cremated where they lay.

The Díaz forces, surrounded in their hideout by Huerta troops, showed no signs of running short of food or ammunition as the terrible farce dragged on. Strange . . . it was almost as if they were getting manna from heaven. Really, of course, they were getting manna from Huerta.

The treacherous general knew that in time the citizens would become so weary of the bloodshed that they would demand the resignation of Madero. When it became plain that the little man from the north could not even control the capital, a strong man could step forward and offer his services. A strong man like Victoriano Huerta . . .

An interesting thing happened as the deadly charade dragged on. The only general Madero could depend on, Felipe Angeles, hurried in from Cuernavaca. After looking over the situation, he decided to attack the *Ciudadela* from another angle. He put his guns in position, then had to deal with a protest from the U.S. ambassador, Henry Lane Wilson. The guns were too near the embassy, Wilson complained; the noise would be disturbing!

Wilson, as it turned out, was part of the Díaz-Huerta plot. The ambassador wanted Félix Díaz as president. Wilson's rich friends in the U.S. had gotten fat under the old Díaz regime. Madero was not cooperating. Another Díaz in the National

During the Tragic Ten Days, civilians carried white flags in combat zone. They died anyway.

Palace was needed to make the rich still richer, so Henry Lane Wilson was doing his best to bring it about.

(The U.S. was not the only foreign government involved. The Japanese took a hand, too, but on the other side. There is evidence that a member of the Japanese legation in Mexico City visited Gustavo Madero as the Tragic Ten Days wore on. The Japanese made an incredible offer. How would it be, the man asked, if 2000 Japanese dressed in white peon cotton attacked the *Ciudadela* in the dark of night? He was sure they could wipe out all the Díaz forces and end the revolt. Gustavo Madero huffily refused the offer. It was a Mexican problem, said Madero, and Mexicans would handle it.)

At last, Huerta, Félix Díaz and Wilson decided to end the bloody masquerade. Huerta began the grim drama of February 18 by inviting Gustavo Madero to lunch. Truly, this is what happened! What's more, Gustavo accepted the invitation. (Remember, it had been Gustavo, the president's brother, who had spoiled the previous plot; Huerta was taking no chances this time.)

While Huerta and Gustavo were lunching, members of the palace guard simply turned their rifles the other way and captured Francisco Madero.

THE MERCY OF HUERTA

Ambassador Wilson sent a joyful message to Washington: "A wicked despotism has fallen!"

The new government was put together in a rather odd place, the U.S. Embassy in Mexico City. The "Compact of the Citadel" called for the placing of Huerta as provisional president until elections could be held, when Félix Díaz would take over.

The sham battle had ended but the grisly days were not over. Gustavo Madero was turned over to the soldiers in the *Ciudadela*. They tortured him before showing the mercy of Huerta and shooting him.

This was not to happen to Francisco Madero. Huerta solemnly agreed that he, Vice-President Pino Suárez and their families could leave for exile in Cuba.

In his cell in the National Palace on the night of February 22, Francisco learned from his mother of the torture and death of Gustavo. The little man cried. At midnight, Madero and Pino Suárez were taken from their cells and put into cars. Their destination was the penitentiary.

At the gates of the prison, they were both shot to death.

The official story from the officers in charge was that an armed mob had attacked them in an attempt to free Madero and Pino Suárez. The two men died in a storm of bullets.

"See?" the officers said, pointing at the automobiles. "They are full of bullet holes, is it not true?"

Ley Fuga, one more time.

So the mild little man from the north, Francisco Madero, failed in his attempt to bring freedom and justice to Mexico. He paid for his failure with his life. It was the same price paid by another gentle man, an Austrian archduke who had tried to rule Mexico almost half a century earlier . . .

History is full of strange little twists. How about this one?

The officer sent to the palace by Huerta to manage the capture of Madero was a certain General Blanquet. This man had been a member of a firing squad on the Hill of the Bells in Querétaro in 1867.

That firing squad, you may remember, was the one which killed Maximilian.

The villain, Victoriano Huerta, glares at a photographer at Fort Bliss, Texas, after being kicked out of Mexico. Is it possible that he slept in his hat?

TEN

--- *The Last Revolution*

"ROOM FOR RENT, BULLET-PROOF . . ."

Zapata, Carranza, Villa, Obregón . . .

Four men lived, four men fought together, then fought each other, killed and finally were killed.

These four are important. These were the last four leaders to fall beside the bloody trail that scorched across the northern deserts, then snaked a fearsome path through the central mountains. The signposts should have read: "This Way to Modern Mexico. WATCH FOR FALLING ROCKS."

When Díaz and Huerta crumpled, the four had time and energy to fight each other. Oh, how they fought! In the fighting, Mexicans and foreigners died. The rich died and the poor died. The rich died violently, quickly; the poor died any way they could, sometimes in an instant, their blood gushing out onto the land they loved. Or they died slowly, their skin stretched over their bones as they starved, the way the poor have always died.

In the last revolution, during the most violent decade of Mexican history, death was democratic. At last, the four leaders

died, all torn apart by bullets. Bugles sound their names along
the musty, echoing halls of history:
EMILIANO ZAPATA . . .
VENUSTIANO CARRANZA . . .
PANCHO VILLA . . .
ALVARO OBREGON . . .

Francisco Madero had promised a new kind of government
for Mexico. He had promised a new life for Mexicans. He could
not deliver. But Mexicans remembered that promises had been
made.

The new president, Victoriano Huerta, could not deliver,
either. He didn't even want to. What he wanted, apparently, was
power, money and time enough to drink all the brandy in Mexico. The 17 months of Huerta's presidency were a disgrace, a disgrace to Mexico, a disgrace to human history.

The decent persons in Huerta's administration soon resigned in disgust. Official robbery and murder happened almost
daily. If you needed to talk to President Huerta, you didn't go
to his office; you searched the drinking places of the city until
you found him. This is true; this is the way it was.

At last, the stink blowing out of Mexico City was too
much. From the north and from the south, the fresh breezes
began to drift. Finally a tornado of revolution swept across the
country.

Two farmers from the north, Carranza and Obregón. A
bandit from the north, Pancho Villa. An Indian farmer from the
south, Emiliano Zapata.

Four different men, with four different goals. Yet somehow they hung together long enough to till the soil and plant
the seeds of modern Mexico.

GARDENS ON THE WATER

Mexico has always been a peasant country, a rural country,
a farming country. Even today, there are only four large cities
--- Mexico City, Guadalajara, Puebla and Monterrey.

First, there were the *chinampas*, the so-called "floating
gardens." Soil was placed on mats floating in a body of fresh
water. More soil was added; often an *ahuehuete* tree was planted

so that its roots would anchor the *chinampa* to solid ground. *Chinampas* were cultivated from small boats floating down the canals between them. The canals were dredged and the solid matter was used to build *chinampas*. An artificial island or peninsula was the result.

For centuries, *chinampas* supplied most of the food for the growing population of the great Valley of Mexico. As late as 1900, Indians paddled canoes along the Canal de la Viga to bring fruits and vegetables to market in the city. Even today, the districts of Xochimilco and Chalco grow vegetables. But most of the lakes and canals have dried up; most of the romance is gone. Dugout canoes once paddled toward market through the warm light of golden mornings; now trucks snort and grind their angry way through smog.

What happened to the *chinampas* as towns grew and needed more space for buildings? They were swallowed up by city people, as farm land has always been swallowed up. Buildings were erected on the *chinampas*. New *chinampas* were formed to produce the food needed by a growing population. These *chinampas*, in turn, became building sites. So it has gone, down the centuries.

This is how Mexico City was able to become the monster of today. Eventually the lakes were drained. Looking at the city of today, with centuries-old buildings tilting every which way, you suspect there must be a better way to build a city.

CORN AND BEANS; BEANS AND CORN
In the deserts of the north and in the uplands farther south, it had to be different. There were few lakes to nourish *chinampas*. But there were still the eternal Mexican sun and the eternal Mexican farmer.

Corn and beans, beans and corn, and a chili pepper here and there. The sun shines from January to January, warming the air, but the rains come only in summer over most of Mexico. The corn patch scratched into the mountainside did well when the rains came. Corn and beans are easy to dry under the lovely sun. Dried corn and beans could carry a family through the waterless winter. But when the rains didn't come . . .

The famous butterflies of Lake Pátzcuaro. Fishermen set out with their graceful nets from island of Janitzio. Statue in background is of Father Morelos.

They call it "subsistence farming." It used to be the way of life for most Mexicans. What it means is that you eat what you grow. If you grow a great plenty, you might be able to sell a little of what you grow.

But everyone needs some cash income, for paying taxes, if nothing else. So you fish or you cut firewood, you make a few baskets, you pot a few pots. Then you load these things on your burro and take them to town on market day. You sit in the sunshine and talk to those who have time to listen; most seem to have time. At the end of the day, if it has been a good day, you pocket a few *pesos*. Perhaps you trade your leftover baskets and pots for a few bananas or limes. Or possibly you trade the *pesos*, too, and go home smiling at your burro because it carries a new blanket, large and heavy, which you know will warm your heart for years of winter nights.

You may say, "It sounds like a good way to live." It was, in a good year. It still is, in a good year. The burros still clop along the Mexican roadsides, carrying their burdens in the patient, plodding way of burros everywhere. The country folk still walk toward town for market day and walk home when the day is over. This may never change.

At Pátzcuaro, on Lake Pátzcuaro in the state of Morelos, some of the old ways remain. An island called Janitzio rises from the lake. On the island live men who fish the lake with nets shaped like butterflies. It is good to live on Janitzio but there is little firewood; nights are cold in winter.

But there is firewood on the mainland. Those who live on the mainland cut wood, then trade wood for fish. The simple barter system has been carried on for centuries. The mainlanders need the good whitefish; the islanders need the firewood. As long as there are fish in the lake and firewood on the mainland, the boats are likely to put out from the island in the morning and the woodcutters will lead their laden burros down to the lakeshore.

In the northwest around Ciudad Obregón, rural life is not so simple. Here, reaching to the horizon, are "factory farms" just as modern as those in California. They are worked by huge machines and sprayed by airplanes. Increasing amounts of these

When these Mayo warriors from northwest Mexico joined General Obregón, they were armed with bows and arrows. Later they were given more modern weapons.

farm products are sold in the U.S. That winter tomato on your dinner table probably grew in the sunshine of Mexico.

In the southeastern Gulf coast states of Veracruz, Chiapas, Tabasco and Yucatán, one sees great cattle ranches and henequen plantations, also as modern as tomorrow.

Yet, not far away, one still can see a farmer toiling in his little corn patch on the mountainside. And still, in the very shadow of the great harvesters and cultivators, a president of Mexico must listen to the age-old peasant cries for land reform.

Land reform was a rallying cry of the Hidalgo revolt in 1810. Yet, when Porfirio Díaz was kicked out of office 100 years later, the situation was as bad as ever; a few thousand persons owned most of Mexico. Francisco Madero stumbled over the problem of land reform. From 1910 to 1920, blood washed over Mexico as peasant armies fought for land reform.

What terrible system of land ownership could cause such outrage to bubble and boil over the years, then finally explode?

It was called "peonage." It wasn't slavery, exactly, but it might as well have been. The owner of the *hacienda*, or farm, was called a *"hacendado."* The *hacendado* didn't hold legal title to his peons, as in slavery.

But that doesn't mean that a peon could just walk off when he felt like it. Peons were paid very little. When they needed food before payday --- which they usually did --- they had to borrow from the *hacendado*. Often they were paid not in *pesos* but in funny money which could be spent only at a store owned by the *hacendado*. The prices at this store, of course, were high.

As a result, peons were in debt to the *hacendado* most of the time. *Hacendados* liked it that way. Debt was the chain which bound the peon to the *hacienda*. If the peon ran away, government police tracked him down and threw him into jail for non-payment of debt. Or shot him down when he tried to escape. *Ley Fuga*, remember?

But how could the government allow this? Easily. Happily. Most government officials were themselves *hacendados*. Even if they weren't, they depended upon *hacendados* for support.

How was it for children in peon families? By age seven, they were working in the fields. There was no teenage time. By age 14, the girls were married, and a year later, they had given birth. The families lived in grim little huts that leaked when it rained; they survived on beans and corn. They had many children. They had to; most of the babies died before they were old enough to work in the fields.

Surviving peon children inherited the debts of their parents. Born in debt; die in debt. Baptism of a baby called for a fiesta. Money to pay for it had to be borrowed from the *hacendado*. A wedding called for another fiesta and more borrowing. Born in debt; die in debt. There seemed to be no way out, except . . .

REVOLUTION!

Some *hacendados* were decent human beings. When the storm broke, some of these were protected from the worst winds.

But most *hacendados* treated peons worse than they treated animals. One of them locked workers into a tiny room each night. The room was so small that the workers had to sleep on top of one another.

The door of this *hacendado's casa* was hand-carved, a thing of great beauty. When the revolution came, this *hacendado's* peons did not protect him from the outrage.

The creature was nailed to his beautiful door. They crucified him and left him to die.

Many landowners operated like kings; the *hacienda* was their kingdom. There is the case of the *hacendado* in Morelos --- Zapata country --- who got angry at a local village. So he turned his irrigation water into a nearby lake. The lake rose and rose, finally flooding the town. In time the only sign that there had been a village at this place was an object rising out of the water --- the spire of the village church!

Pancho Villa was a peon who escaped and who never forgot his peonage. Emiliano Zapata rode into history leading an army of peons. They committed outrages, but their terrible anger was honestly come by.

Pancho Villa's soldiers enter Ciudad Juárez in 1912. You'll note that it's not easy to tell soldiers from civilians.

BACK TO THE MONSTER

You may remember that we left the Mexican government in the hands of a monster, Victoriano Huerta.

What Huerta wanted was to bring back the sweet days of Porfirio Díaz, when the rich got richer and the poor got shot at. U.S. Ambassador Henry Lane Wilson thought this was a fine idea, as did his boss back in Washington, D.C., President William Howard Taft. European businessmen saw Huerta as a promising tyrant, too. Germany, especially, had invested heavily in Mexico. German interests, familiar with military rule under the kaisers, thought it would be just great if Mexico could have a home-grown kaiser. Great for German profits, that is.

But Huerta was no Díaz. He was a military man and a drunk, nothing more. Official duties bored him, so he spent very little time in the National Palace, much more time in saloons.

This was often a nuisance to the powerful men who had put Huerta in office, but President Huerta could be trusted not to come up with silly notions like land reform, honest elections, and "Mexico for the Mexicans."

However, Huerta was haunted by a ghost. The ghost looked suspiciously like Francisco Madero. Maybe Huerta didn't order the murder of Madero but he didn't stop it, either.

The mark of Madero was on him.

The winds which had blown Madero into office were still stirring up the deserts of the north, still whistling through the canyons of the south. In the northeastern state of Coahuila, a white-bearded man named Venustiano Carranza ran the show. His territory was close to Texas. This was important, because no Mexican revolution in modern times has succeeded without U.S. support. Mostly the revolutionists needed guns and ammunition. If a U.S. president chose to shut down gun-running, he shut down the revolution. If a U.S. president let the guns flow, he caused earthquakes in the National Palace.

In the days of Díaz, Carranza had been a senator. He was a patriot, but he was also a narrow-minded, stubborn, snobbish man. He thought of himself as the only man who could save Mexico. Early in the game, he began to call himself "First Chief."

He said that he wanted to wipe out Huerta. What he really wanted, though, was to sit in that fancy chair in the National Palace. And sit there and sit there . . .

VILLA RIDES!

"Doroteo Arango" --- that was the real name, the peon name, of the wild, colorful, loving, hating, tragic, humorous giant of Mexican history known better as Francisco "Pancho" Villa. He started as a peon, then became a cowboy. He fled the *hacienda* at age 16, after killing the *hacendado*'s son for raping Villa's sister. He became a bandit. Mostly he stole from Luis Terrazas, a super-rich landowner. This was necessary because Terrazas owned almost everything in Villa's part of Mexico. (A U.S. meat company once cabled Terrazas to ask if he could deliver 15,000 cattle immediately. Terrazas cabled back: "What color?") Villa became a revolutionary, then a clever general of armies who dreamed up new ways to win battles. For a time, his Army of the North was unbeatable. He did not want to become president of Mexico . . . he said. What he wanted, he said, was justice for peons.

For ten years, the cry of "Villa rides!" could collect and fire up an army in a matter of weeks. For one brief moment, just for fun, he sat in the president's chair in the National Palace, the chair he said he didn't want. He could not fill the chair. He knew it.

Emiliano Zapata always knew what he wanted. So did the tens of thousands of his followers. Land, their own land --- nothing more, nothing less. Let others worry about throwing out the foreigners, honest elections or cleaning up corruption in the capital.

As a young man in the state of Morelos, Zapata showed great talent as a handler of horses. As a result, the *hacendado*'s stables were open to him. Zapata didn't have to look very hard to see that the *hacendado*'s horses lived better than his peons. This grim truth burned within the man for the rest of his life.

Zapata enjoyed some early success as a village politician working within the system. The Díaz dictatorship was showing signs of rot. The Madero forces were rising in the north; nervous

For a moment, at least, Pancho Villa sat in Mexico's presidential chair. This picture was a little joke, nothing more. That's Emiliano Zapata at his left, with the big hat. Neither was cut out for life in the big city. Both soon left for their old haunts, Villa heading north and Zapata south.

These were soldiers of the revolution between 1910 and 1920. Third from left is probably older than he looks. Note the rifles; no two are alike. Imagine the problem of supplying ammunition for this fierce group.

landowners were willing to give the young Zapata and his peon followers a few small victories. In 1910, with the Madero forces chopping hard at the Díaz regime, Zapata turned revolutionary.

As a general, Zapata added something new to Mexican warfare --- the disappearing army. Zapata's peons swept like avenging ghosts over the state of Morelos, looting and burning *haciendas* and killing *hacendados*. When Federal troops charged out from Mexico City to punish them, Zapata's soldiers seemed to vanish into thin air. They dressed in white cotton, wide-brimmed hats and sandals, as peons always had, instead of in military uniforms. To disappear, all a *Zapatista* had to do was hide his rifle and ammunition belt under the nearest bush. When the Federals rode by, they saw a simple peasant working in a cane field or squatting by the roadside.

Then, when the call went out from their leader, the ghosts gathered up their arms; suddenly there was an army again.

Federal generals usually went back to the capital grinding their teeth in frustration. *Caramba!* How is an army supposed to fight an enemy it can't find?

There was no mistaking General Zapata, though. His slim figure was clothed in a black *charro* costume, sparkling with silver. His white sombrero was enormous. His dark eyes flashed over a sweeping moustache. He rode a white horse.

"Land!" was the cry of the *Zapatistas*. Then, like the scream of an attacking hawk: "DEATH TO THE HACENDADOS!"

Emiliano Zapata had no wish to be president of Mexico. He might have accepted the governorship of the state of Morelos, but no more. He hated the corruption of the capital, never stayed there a moment longer than necessary. The poison never touched him. From the bright beginning to the terrible end, he stayed clean despite the mud flying all around him.

The last revolution swept down from the north. Emiliano Zapata was always a man of the south. He could not be a national leader. His Mexico was Morelos, his people were the peasant farmers. He trusted them, not the man in power in Mexico City. They trusted him and even today, in the beautiful state of

This poster rather makes it sound like an expense-paid vacation, doesn't it? You can almost read between the lines: "Spend weekends in exotic Acapulco!" Actually, some gringos who went south thought of the experience as fun and games. Or, as the poster puts it: "Gold and Glory."

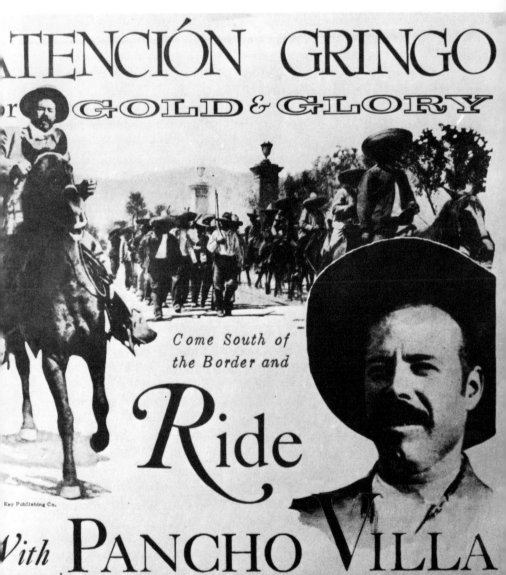

ATENCIÓN GRINGO
or GOLD & GLORY

Come South of
the Border and

Ride

Key Publishing Co.

With PANCHO VILLA

El Liberator of Mexico!

WEEKLY PAYMENTS IN GOLD TO
DYNAMITERS ♦ MACHINE GUNNERS ♦ RAILROADERS

Enlistments Taken In Juarez, Mexico
♦ *January 1915* ♦

VIVA VILLA! VIVA Revolución!

236

Morelos, there are those working in the fields who will tell you softly that Emiliano Zapata is not dead. How could such a man die?

OBREGON THE IRISHMAN

The last Spanish viceroy of Mexico had an Irish bodyguard named Michael O'Brien. Naturally, this name soon became "Miguel Obregón."

This explains the rosy cheeks and tipped-up nose of Alvaro Obregón, of the northern state of Sonora. It may also explain his sense of humor.

As a small farmer with a young family, he did not join the Madero rebellion; there are signs that he wished later that he had. But when the Madero presidency went sour, he turned rebel.

He lacked the boldness and flair of Villa and Zapata but he was wiser and more flexible than Carranza. Sonora and Chihuahua were the launching pads of the last revolution; Sonora was Obregón country. It was also Yaqui Indian country. Yaquis became the strong center of Obregón's army. No surprise there; Yaquis had a reputation as the most fierce fighters in all of Mexico.

The Díaz government had stolen Yaqui land early in its rule, starting about 1880. *Rurales* were sent in, Yaquis were killed and the survivors were resettled. But, when they were squeezed again, the Yaquis rebelled. Furious, President Díaz ordered that the Yaquis be wiped out.

Any soldier, snarled Díaz, who brought in a Yaqui's ears would be paid about $30. Many bonuses were paid but who can tell a Yaqui by his ears?

In 1892, the entire Yaqui population of the Sonora town of Navajoa was jailed. So many were hanged that the town's supply of rope was used up. During that same year, 200 Yaquis were forced into a boat at the Sonora port of Guaymas and drowned in the sea.

Still the Yaquis fought back. Between 1898 and 1908, the Díaz government shipped Yaquis by the thousands to subtropical Yucatán and to southern Mexico.

Ten to 20 per cent usually died along the way. Sixty to 70 per cent died during the first year of their slavery on the henequen plantations. In 1908, a shipload of Yaquis bound for Yucatán took the easy way out --- suicide. The officer in charge, Colonel Francisco B. Cruz, said:

"Those Indians wanted to cheat us out of our commission money and so they threw their children into the sea and jumped in after them. We lowered boats but it was no use; they all went down before we got to them."

By 1910, only the strongest and smartest of the Yaqui race had managed to survive in Sonora. These were the hard core of Obregón's conquering army. They had always fought for good reason. With each passing year of the Díaz dictatorship, they had better reasons. They were invincible.

Obregón was the single man among the four who led the last revolution who could rule as well as fight, who knew the country and how to lead it.

But who died too soon, cut down by bullets just like the others.

The Huerta administration probably was doomed in the instant that a new U.S. president, Woodrow Wilson, decided that Mexico needed a new government. Arms and supplies again began to flow across the border to the rebel armies, who called themselves "Constitutionalists."

The Big Four were united mostly by their hatred of Huerta. First Chief Carranza was no military leader but he stubbornly tried to control military decisions. Pancho Villa was a natural leader of troops but his hot temper and erratic nature frequently got him into trouble. Calm, clever Alvaro Obregón often was the man in the middle; he supplied the glue which held the campaign together. In the south, Emiliano Zapata did his own thing. One might say that he was the bottom half of the pincers which squeezed Huerta.

Pancho Villa quickly discovered a new way to fight a war in Mexico. A 1300-kilometer rail line reached from Chihuahua City to Mexico City; why not move an army that way? Villa loved horses but horses couldn't gallop all day and all night, nor could they carry much. Steam locomotives could chuff away

Railroads in Mexico took a terrible beating during the years 1910-1920. Here Constitutionalists destroy a bridge to slow down a Federalist advance.

Another way to go to war. Villa's soldiers and their families often lived on top of railroad cars.

day and night, hauling behind them horses, soldiers, guns and supplies. Tracks could be blown up, of course, but trains could carry repair crews, too.

A Villa army on the move looked like a mob fleeing a disaster. But this mob might very well be singing its theme song, *"La Cucaracha."* Soldiers and their families were stacked three deep in the cars; those left over built blanket tents on top of boxcars. A few young *bravos* even slung hammocks underneath the cars and rode among the clattering wheels!

Some women in Villa's army were fighting soldiers; others were wives and mothers, travelling along to take care of their families. Villa's army was expected to live off the land, so the women scoured the countryside for food and did their cooking where they could. Some hardy women even set up kitchens on the front platforms of locomotives, built fires there and baked tortillas!

It was a peculiar way to run a railroad --- or an army. At times, all those people got in the way. For quick, bold strokes away from the rail line, General Villa needed cavalry. He organized and trained the soon-to-be-famous *Dorados;* these hard-riding horsemen became the sharp point of Villa's lance. (Their name grew out of the gold decorations on their olive uniforms.)

Since most of the Federal strongpoints were along the Chihuahua-Mexico City rail line, Villa's forces had to fight the really hard battles. It seemed only fair that it should be Pancho Villa who entered Mexico City in triumph.

First Chief Carranza said, in effect, "Over my dead body."

Carranza ordered Villa's army west to Zacatecas. Furious, General Villa resigned. The First Chief happily accepted his resignation.

Villa's officers sent angry messages to Carranza. They accused the First Chief of blocking Villa's road to Mexico City; they demanded that Carranza put Villa back in command. Carranza refused.

Then Pancho realized that he had done a dumb thing. So he pretended that nothing had happened. He ordered his army to Zacatecas. The town was taken after a bloody battle.

Villa wrote: "Later reports confirmed my estimate that out of 12,000 defenders of Zacatecas no more than 200 escaped... The next day at nine in the morning I entered Zacatecas... Those who came out to meet me, men, women and children, had to leap over the corpses to greet me. Beside the enemy dead many of my soldiers lay resting, sleeping in pools of blood."

But Villa did not capture the one item he needed most --- coal for his locomotives. Carranza controlled the coal supply. Villa got none of it. As Obregón's forces raced into Mexico City, *La Cucaracha* was stalled at Zacatecas.

The break between Villa and Carranza was final.

U.S. President Woodrow Wilson, disgusted by Huerta, wanted to help the Carranza forces even more than he already had. In the spring of 1914, a few sailors from an American warship landed in a forbidden area near Tampico on the Gulf coast. They were arrested by Federal soldiers. An hour and a half later, the sailors were released with an apology.

What excitement in Washington! To make things right, the Yankees bellowed, Mexicans would have to deliver a 21-gun salute to the U.S. flag.

President Huerta said, *"No, señores."*

So President Wilson sent the U.S. fleet into the Gulf of Mexico. On April 21, a message was flashed that the German ship *Ypiranga* was headed for Veracruz with munitions for Huerta.

"Seize Veracruz," ordered Wilson. It was done. In the process, 200 Mexican defenders lost their lives. The capture of Veracruz served no useful purpose; Huerta got the German munitions anyway. But *gringos* had another black mark in the Mexican mind.

After the panicky flight of Victoriano Huerta, who would sit in the president's chair? Defeating Huerta seemed to have solved nothing. Now the Big Four were fighting each other.

Carranza and Villa were hopelessly split. Obregón dashed around negotiating with his powerful friends and with Pancho Villa. To them, Carranza was not acceptable as president. Yet, to the *Carranzistas*, no one but Carranza was acceptable.

How about Pancho Villa, the motorcyclist? He probably would have fit right in with Hell's Angels.

In an attempt to hammer out an agreement, a great convention was scheduled for Aguascalientes in October, 1914. Carranza refused to attend; he had wanted the convention in Mexico City, where he could control it. After weeks of arguing, the convention nominated a general, Eulalio Gutiérrez, as provisional president.

Pancho Villa may have come up with the best idea of the convention. Since the fight between the *Villistas* and the *Carranzistas* seemed to be the big problem, why, Pancho suggested, didn't he and Carranza commit suicide? And Villa may have hated Carranza enough to go through with it . . .

Now Alvaro Obregón had to choose between the "Convention" president and Carranza. He chose Carranza. This left Gutiérrez no choice but to ask Villa for military support. When it appeared that Villa would be moving on the capital, Carranza decided to take his government to Veracruz for safekeeping. Meanwhile the new leader of the Carranza armies, General Obregón, would teach the bandit from the north a few things about fighting.

Obregón had an idea. Villa would attack; he always did. This time, though, *Los Dorados* might get a surprise.

BACK TO BANDITRY

Villa's attack strategy failed miserably when Obregón's armies fought from trenches protected by barbed wire. This was European-style fighting, new to Mexico. Corpses of the once-proud *Dorados* soon hung on the barbed wire by the hundreds, then by the thousands. Some of Villa's most trusted officers deserted, along with many soldiers. When President Wilson, in October, 1915, cut off Villa's U.S. arms supply, the glory days of the *Villistas* were over. Pancho had started his wild career as a *bandido;* now he was a *bandido* again.

But just once more he would make a big splash in the newspapers. In March of 1916, Villa led a reckless raid into the little border town of Columbus, New Mexico. His 400 men were fought off by soldiers stationed at the town. However, 18 Americans were killed.

It was the excuse President Wilson was waiting for. He immediately sent General John J. Pershing on a wild goose chase across the border in pursuit of *Villistas*.

Like most U.S. military adventures in Mexico, this one failed. Instead of destroying Pancho Villa, the silly expedition made him a hero again. (It is entirely possible that this is what the sly Villa had in mind when he raided Columbus.) If the U.S. gained anything, it was the knowledge that its army was in sad shape. With a really big war looming against Germany, this was good to know.

Meanwhile, back in the capital, President Carranza was having his problems. Since he would not take the advice of the good people around him, the good people were leaving. Among these, finally, was Alvaro Obregón, the last anchor of his government.

Forced to call a constitutional convention in late 1916, Carranza found that his claws had been pulled. Two hardheaded generals ran the show, Obregón and Francisco Múgica.

Since Carranza didn't believe in the resulting constitution, he didn't try to make it work. By the end of 1918, Carranza had lost most of his old supporters and had picked up few new ones. With his term nearing its end, he might have slipped safely into retirement. Not this stubborn old man. Since, under the constitution, he could not succeed himself, Carranza looked for a puppet. Stupidly, he chose an unknown, Ignacio Bonillas.

Obregón pronounced against Carranza. A cheering nation made Obregón's march to Mexico City little more than a noisy parade.

But Obregón's victory had come too late for one great Mexican hero --- Emiliano Zapata.

President Carranza felt that he had two major enemies --- Villa and Zapata. In Carranza's mind, these two were bandits and killers. Uncivilized brutes, nothing more. So Carranza's army spent most of its time chasing Zapata and Villa. Especially Zapata.

It was embarrassing to have Emiliano tearing up the state of Morelos, so close to the capital. The president sent General

Execution by firing squad was routine in Mexico during the years of horror. This one took place near Ciudad Juárez. Note spectators at left.

Pablo González to Morelos with orders to destroy everything that hadn't already been destroyed. (González had already gained fame as the Carranza general who had never won a battle. However, he was very good at killing unarmed civilians.)

González burned villages. He destroyed crops. He hanged all the men he could capture, then herded women and children into concentration camps. But he did not wipe out Zapata . . .

It had to be done by treachery. Colonel Jesús Guajardo was assigned to the job. Word was passed to Zapata that Guajardo and his 800 soldiers, with all their arms and ammunition, were ready to desert Carranza and join the *Zapatistas*.

Zapata was suspicious, but accepted Guajardo's offer.

The government held the town of Jonacatepec. Attack this town, said Zapata, and capture the soldiers.

Guajardo sent his army against the town, killing many of its defenders. When the fight was over, he ordered the survivors shot.

Zapata and Guajardo agreed to meet at San Juan Chinameca.

Bugles sounded a salute as Zapata arrived at the *hacienda* with ten of his officers. In the courtyard, a guard of honor waited.

"Present arms!"

The rifles rose --- and fired, riddling Zapata and his officers.

But in Morelos, the legend of Zapata, the black-clad leader on the white horse, still rides the hills in the light of the moon.

How could such a man die?

Carranza, hearing of Obregón's swift march from the north, decided to flee to Veracruz. But the departure was delayed for a few days, because Carranza's people were taking everything in the capital that wasn't nailed down, loading things like kitchen stoves and wardrobes into cars and hauling them to the railroad station.

The trains waited, and waited, while the plundering went on. At last, on May 7, the presidential train, plus 30 others, groaned out of Mexico City. There were 10,000 persons aboard but no medical supplies nor water. There was no space for these things; Carranza's greedy followers had even stolen the light fixtures from the National Palace!

The trains were attacked again and again as they fled with their loot. Carranza finally became so frightened that he left his train and fled northward in the state of Puebla, trudging along mountain trails through heavy rain.

On May 20, an exhausted President Carranza was put to bed in a thatched hut in a little village, his head on a saddle, his only cover a horse blanket. His guide and "protector," a local chieftain named Rodolfo Herrero, had assured the president that he would be safe.

Herrero arranged an attack on the hut just before dawn. Gunfire killed Carranza. The attackers also stole the president's pistols, his spectacles, his typewriter and his watch.

So in the end, Carranza had to pay for the light fixtures.

Pancho Villa was next. In 1920, the government had bought him off with a large parcel of land near the northern town of Parral. Still in his early forties, Villa seemed to settle down to the life of country squire. (One might even have called him a *hacendado*.)

But Villa enjoyed this quiet life --- if he did enjoy it --- less than three years. His enemies were like flies in summer; he could not watch them all.

On July 20, 1923, Villa was leaving Parral at the wheel of his Dodge touring car to return to his *hacienda*.

The first gunfire blasted from the buildings along the street. Then a few men charged the car, which had left the street and struck a tree.

The cry of "Villa rides!" would never again echo across the deserts of northern Mexico.

Oh, the stories they tell about Pancho Villa! No writer can let him die without telling them once again.

Once Pancho Villa was trying to take Chihuahua City from the Federals but found it too difficult. He really would rather have taken Ciudad Juárez, anyway, since this town was the most important along the entire border. But since the tracks from the

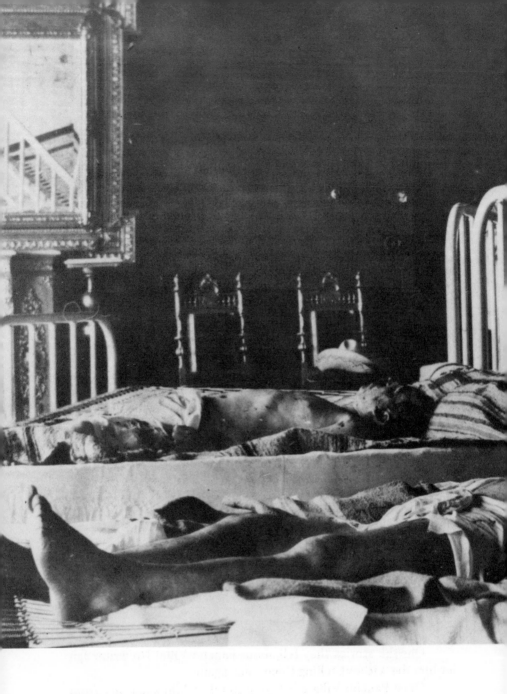

This photograph was taken in a Parral hotel not long after the assassination of Pancho Villa. The revolutionary general is in the near bed, an aide in the bed beyond.

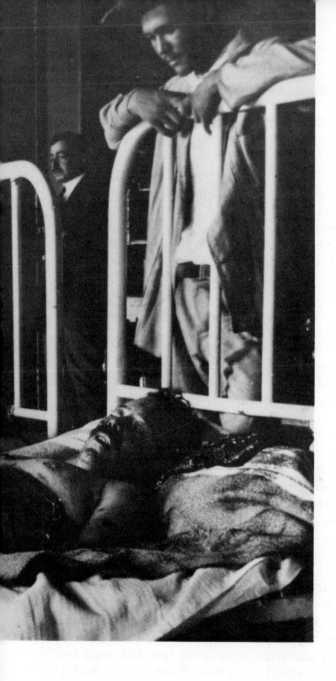

south ran through Chihuahua City, how could he take his trains to Juárez?

He couldn't, of course. So he picked 2000 of his best soldiers and circled Chihuahua at a safe distance. And then he had a bit of luck.

Headed toward Chihuahua was a Federal coal train. Villa's men attacked it and captured it, along with its telegrapher.

A pistol pointed at the head of the telegrapher encouraged him to send a message in official code to Ciudad Juárez: "LINE TO JUAREZ BURNED BY REVOLUTIONARIES. SEND REPAIR ENGINE AND ORDERS."

Return message: "NO REPAIR ENGINES AVAILABLE."

Villa then warned Ciudad Juárez through his captive telegrapher that he had spotted a dust cloud on the horizon which looked like rebels on the march.

Quickly Ciudad Juárez ordered the train to return.

At midnight the Trojan horse train slipped into Ciudad Juárez with the Federals asleep at the switch. Villa's troops leaped off in the center of town and by dawn, this most important border town was in Villa's hands. Not a single Villa soldier had been lost in the fight!

Villa could be cruel; he had a temper. Oh, what a temper Villa had! Once he was being interviewed by an American newspaperman. A drunken soldier began to yell outside the window. Without interrupting his reply to the reporter's question, Villa went to the window, drew his pistol and gunned down his own soldier.

A man like Pancho Villa always had plenty of enemies. Men just as cruel as he, who would kill just as quickly. (And maybe a few women, too; he married at least four times, without bothering to divorce anybody.) But anyone who wanted to kill Villa knew that he would have to make his first shot count because the second shot would come from Pancho's gun. And it wouldn't miss . . .

Born in peonage, bred in banditry, Villa lived in suspicion. He would choose a place to sleep for the night, then would change it. Instead of eating with his officers, Villa would pass among his troops, taking a bite from one soldier's plate, a bite from another's. To poison Villa, it would have been necessary to poison his entire army. No man was braver in battle than Pancho Villa; no man took more precautions to insure that he would live to fight another day. But Villa, like so many other of his brothers in violence, would one day have to pay his dues.

SMILE WHEN YOU SAY "GRINGO"

Greasers and *gringos* . . .

This is the way it used to be along the U.S.-Mexico border. You don't hear "greaser" much any more, and *"gringo"* isn't the swear word it once was. These days, even *gringos* call themselves *gringos*.

There were Mexicans, remember, who died in the Alamo, fighting alongside *gringos*. Benito Juárez was --- and is --- a U.S. hero, too. So is --- and may God help the old cutthroat --- Pancho Villa. The revolution of 1910-1920, out of which grew modern Mexican government, was helped mightily by U.S. support --- and damaged only a little by U.S. blundering.

It took the U.S. government a long time to learn that Mexico wanted to handle its own problems, with a little help from its friends. What it did NOT want was U.S. troops charging into Chihuahua and U.S. ships blasting away at Veracruz, no matter how noble the intentions.

Seems reasonable, when you think about it.

U.S. politicians and businessmen often supported tyrants like Porfirio Díaz and Victoriano Huerta. But there were many ordinary *gringos*, especially along the border, who believed that the brutes should be bounced.

When Francisco Madero was trying to get his act together against Díaz, he needed U.S. help badly. The U.S. government had a heavy investment in the Díaz dictatorship. The politicians of the dollar sign weren't about to switch to Madero.

But *gringos* in the El Paso-Juárez neighborhood sent support to Madero by throwing silver dollars across a narrow stretch of the Rio Grande River!

Nothing but foreign aid, the quick and easy way.

U.S. citizens living along the border had a very personal interest in the ebb and flow of revolution. They could hardly help it; every once in a while bullets whistled around their ears.

This was especially true in El Paso, Texas, only a river's width away from Ciudad Juárez. It was also true in Douglas, Arizona, just across the border from Agua Prieta. During the long years of revolution, these key points were fought over again and again.

By the end of 1914, one U.S. civilian had been killed and 14 wounded in Naco, a little town on the Arizona border. In Naco, as well as in other border towns, hotelkeepers began to advertise "bullet-proof rooms." It's true; it happened.

The border fighting gave birth to a new kind of social function called "battle teas." Hostesses with well-located, flat-roofed houses invited guests to watch the afternoon's fighting from the roof. Tea and cakes were served; guests were asked to bring their own binoculars. All this is true; it actually happened along the border during the years of revolution.

ARTIST WITH A GUN

Alvaro Obregón had become president in 1920. He ruled firmly, as everyone knew he would, but without the wholesale brutality of Díaz. During his four-year term, more than 12,000 hectares (about three million acres) of land were returned to peasant ownership. At long last, land reform was becoming a reality in Mexico.

Obregón's term was noted, too, for improvement of education. The president had the good sense to appoint a brilliant person, José Vasconcelos, as minister of education. Training teachers and opening schools throughout the country, Vasconcelos made his mark as Mexico's greatest educator.

To follow himself as president, Obregón wanted Plutarco Calles, who had been a loyal officer in the old days in Sonora. After a small rebellion had been crushed, Calles was elected. Four years later, Calles wanted to pass the job back to Obregón. There was muttering about this and once more, a mini-revolution had to be stamped out. Old habits die hard.

Three weeks after he had been elected to his second term, Alvaro Obregón was enjoying dinner at a restaurant in San Angel. A young religious fanatic, José de León Toral, entered the restaurant and began to draw portraits of the diners. He came close to Obregón and began to sketch him.

Then he snatched out a pistol and shot . . .

Alvaro Obregón, the fourth leader of the last great revolution, died like the others, his life ripped out by bullets.

Alvaro Obregón was not a Benito Juárez but once again, Mexico had lost a wise leader too soon.

Five minutes after this photograph was taken, Alvaro Obregón (with beard, at center) was shot and killed.

This unusual church of pink stone was designed by an Indian architect, Cerefino Gutiérrez, during the 19th century. It is in San Miguel de Allende, state of Guanajuato.

ELEVEN
--- The Church

"ARE YOU NOT UNDER MY SHADOW AND PROTECTION?"

Each day of the year, pilgrims from all over Mexico are drawn to this particular church in a northern district of Mexico City. Some drop to their knees and creep across many meters of concrete between the busy street and the church. They enter the basilica, still on their knees. They do not seem to notice the pain.

What draws them here? Why do hundreds of thousands each year spend many pesos to journey here for worship?

They come because this is the Basilica of Guadalupe. They come because hanging over the altar in this church is a small painting of a Virgin. Not just an ordinary Virgin. This Virgin, unlike all the others, has dark skin, Indian skin. This is the Black Madonna, the most sacred religious object in all of Mexico.

And now you must hear the legend of the Virgin of Guadalupe.

His race was Aztec; his age was 57. His Indian name was Cuauhtlatoahuac, or "Singing Eagle." Baptized into Christianity, he became "Juan Diego." As Juan Diego, he is now a towering

Across the enormous Zócalo, main plaza of Mexico City, towers the National Cathedral. A pedestrian prays before and after crossing the street.

figure in Mexican history. Whatever seemed to happen to this peasant in the early morning mists of December 9, 1531, is still accepted as truth by millions of Mexican Catholics.

Juan Diego was on his way to mass at Tlatelolco. At the foot of a low, rocky hill near the village of Tepeyac, he heard a voice say in the Indian tongue, "Son Juan, where are you going?"

Even though he was startled, he was able to answer. Then he noticed that the entire hill shone with a strange light. He heard the song of birds but saw no birds. When the voice beckoned, he went up the hill.

At the top he saw the Virgin, bathed in light!

Speaking always in Juan Diego's language, the Virgin told him that she wanted her sanctuary built on that very hill. He was to carry the Virgin's request to the bishop, Juan de Zumárraga.

He was not accustomed to talking to bishops, but he had to do what the Virgin asked of him.

The bishop was not impressed. The Virgin appearing before this ragged old peasant? Not likely. But the bishop did say that if the Virgin would send a sign, he might change his mind.

Juan Diego returned home through the dark of night, only to find that he had more trouble; his uncle was very ill. After staying at his uncle's bedside through the night, Juan Diego left at dawn to get a priest for the last sacraments. His uncle was about to die. He avoided the hill of Tepeyac, taking a path along the lakeshore.

But he could not escape; he saw the Virgin coming down the hill toward him. Juan Diego begged to leave.

The Virgin said, "Let nothing alter your heart or your countenance. Am I not your Mother? Are you not under my shadow and protection? Are you not in the crossing of my arms?"

The Virgin said she would give him a sign for the bishop. They climbed to the top of the hill. There, to Juan Diego's great surprise, roses bloomed where only cactus had grown before!

Following the Virgin's instructions, Juan Diego picked some roses, then handed them to her. The Virgin enfolded the flowers in Juan Diego's cloak, which was made of maguey fibers.

Then she said, "This is the sign which you are to give to the Lord Bishop. You are my ambassador, worthy of my confidence. Do not let anyone see what you are carrying. Do not unfold the cloak until you are in his presence."

Once again Juan Diego hurried off to see the bishop. This time there was new hope in his heart. But when he opened his cloak to show the roses to the bishop, they were gone!

Instead of the flowers, there was a painting of the Virgin on the cloak.

MIRACLE, INDIAN STYLE

A small chapel was built on the hill of Tepeyac; mass was said before the wonderful painting. Later a basilica was built at the foot of the hill. The painting of the Virgin of Guadalupe, encased in a frame of gold, silver and bronze, was placed over the altar. There it rests today, glowing under many lights and quickly drawing the attention of all who enter the basilica.

Only one and one-half meters tall, the painting has one remarkable feature: the dark skin of the Virgin. The skin of an Indian . . .

The largest church in Mexico is the National Cathedral, which dominates the north side of the Zócalo in Mexico City. (In fact, it is the largest church in North or South America.) This enormous pile of stone might be called the "establishment" church. The church of the plain people of Mexico --- and of some not so plain --- is the Basilica of Guadalupe.

Almost three centuries after Juan Diego's miracle, Father Hidalgo led the revolt against the Spanish. The priest knew what image had to be on the banner carried by his marchers: the Virgin of Guadalupe.

So you don't believe in miracles? You aren't alone. There are those in Mexico and elsewhere who point to the fact that after the "miracle" occurred, Bishop Zumárraga and his priests found it much easier to convert Indians to Catholicism.

Fact or legend? Perhaps it doesn't matter. As long as there are Catholics in Mexico, they will drop to their knees and bring flowers to their dark-skinned Madonna. As they creep toward

The new shrine of Guadalupe as it nears completion. This one holds 10,000 persons and is guaranteed not to sink.

This is the great Cholula pyramid, with Catholic church on top and restoration work in progress in foreground.

the basilica, some will turn aside to avoid rough patches of concrete. Others will bring assistants to lay down mats to ease the pain. But still they come.

HOW MANY CHURCHES?

One needs to travel only a few hours in Mexico to begin thinking of it as a land of churches. The towering spires mark the villages from many kilometers away. (One town, Cholula, is said to have 365 churches, one for each day of the year. This is nonsense. Possibly if one stood on the Cholula pyramid on a clear day, one could see 365 church spires in the surrounding Puebla valley. Even this is doubtful, though. So you see, tourist promoters need their legends, too.)

Nearly all of the churches are Catholic. Mexico, after all, is a Catholic country. The Spanish, starting with Cortés and company, took care of that.

The priests let very little grass grow under their sandals. In 1522, the first three Spanish priests arrived at Tlaxcala and went to work. Two years later, a dozen more Franciscans arrived at Veracruz and proceeded to do an astonishing thing. They walked through the terrible mountains between Veracruz and Mexico City --- 480 kilometers --- barefoot!

It was a great entrance; everybody who saw them was bowled over. The soldier of Cortés, Bernal Díaz, wrote:

"When Cuauhtémoc and the other *caciques* saw Cortés fall to his knees and kiss the friars' hands, their astonishment was very great. And when they saw that the friars were barefoot and thin, and that their habits were ragged, and that they did not ride horseback, but walked, and were very pale; and when they saw Cortés, whom they considered an idol or something like their gods, thus kneeling, all the Indians followed his example, so that now, when the friars come, the Indians receive them with the same reverence and respect."

All Saints Day is only one of many religious holidays on the Mexican calendar. The place of this observance is unrecorded but a good guess would be the island of Janitzio in Lake Pátzcuaro.

There were two kinds of priests in Mexico --- independent and secular. There were three large independent orders --- Franciscan, Dominican and Augustinian. (Of the small orders, perhaps the most important was the Jesuit.) Members of independent orders were also called "mendicants." That is, beggars. They supported their work by begging.

They were called "independent" for a very good reason; no government could lay a finger on them. They owed their only allegiance to the Pope in Rome. Under the right called *fuero*, they paid no taxes and did not have to obey most civil laws. They were, in fact, a law unto themselves. They conducted their own trials and even their own executions.

The members of the secular orders, on the other hand, were citizens like anyone else. Well . . . almost.

Can you imagine the trouble caused by this arrangement? Admission to the mendicant orders required great dedication and long training, so naturally, the mendicants looked down on the seculars. The seculars, of course, envied and resented the special privileges of the mendicants. This led to one squabble after another.

Some of the most intelligent and forceful leaders in Mexico were mendicant priests and bishops. Bishop Zumárraga, already mentioned, was a Franciscan. So was Father Junípero Serra, who limped along on a sore leg through an incredible journey to California, thus extending the influence of Mexico all the way to San Francisco Bay.

Possibly the greatest of them all was Vasco de Quiroga, a Dominican. He became Bishop of Michoacán. He taught the Indians, he protected them from persecution, he built a small City of God by the water under the sun of Michoacán. Even today, this man is worshipped as a saint by the residents of that beautiful lake country.

Father Kino, the great explorer and colonizer in the northern deserts, was a Jesuit. His name lives on in a Sonora town 90 kilometers south of the Arizona border, Magdalena de Kino. Father Kino's skeleton lies in an open grave in the center of town. In this area of Mexico, any object that this great man is known to have touched is a treasured relic.

FIRST, LET'S TALK

The first hurdle to be leaped by the early priests was language. Many of them learned Indian tongues, then taught Spanish to Indians. In their spare time, they did their best to wipe out all traces of Indian religions. Pyramids were torn apart, temples burned and records destroyed. In some cases, temples were removed from pyramids, then replaced by Catholic churches.

This made sense to the Indians, since it had been their normal practice to build a new pyramid on top of an old one. The most striking example of this is at Cholula, where a Catholic church towers over the countryside on top of seven old pyramids!

The priests worked so hard at destroying all signs of ancient Mexican cultures that they threatened to lose the rich record forever. Before that point was reached, however, an interesting thing happened. Priests had destroyed, now other priests would work as hard to save what was left. One of the most important in this effort was Bernardino de Sahagún, but there were many others. What we know of old Mexico today, we owe to them.

(It should be remembered that Bishop Juan de Zumárraga made another strong contribution to the culture. He brought the first pair of burros to Mexico. If rural Mexicans could choose a National Animal, the burro surely would win hands down.)

It's easy to find things to criticize in the work of the mendicant orders in Mexico. But they are beyond criticism in one area --- energy.

For instance, the first Augustinians arrived in Mexico in 1533. One of their leaders, Fray Toribio de Motolinïa, estimated that in their first 15 years, Augustinians baptized no less than nine million Indians!

That figure may be higher than truth. But the fact remains that Mexico, only 50 years after the Spanish conquest, had become a Catholic country. What the Catholic missionaries did, to put it simply, was work themselves out of a job.

So then they settled back to enjoy the fruits of their labor. Convents and churches of great size and golden splendor began to thrust their proud spires into the skies of Mexico. The skinny,

One of the most valuable contributions of Spanish churchmen to Mexico was the burro. Burros have trained many muchachos like this one.

barefoot friars who had walked across the mountains from Veracruz were followed by fat, luxury-loving tyrants. Indians paid
for the buildings and the lush living, first with their bits of
money, then with their unpaid labor.

When complaints were heard, the friars and the bishops
had a standard answer: "All for the glory of God."

The independent orders did most of the early missionary
work. But there weren't nearly enough independents to staff all
the new churches. Secular priests, under the control of the government, filled the gaps. All *haciendas*, except the smallest, had
their own priests. Every mining operation of any size had a
priest; the large mines had several. Eventually there were more
than 8000 secular priests in Mexico.

If the church didn't quite run the country, it owned it . . .
almost. A respected historian, Lucas Alamán, estimated that
after three centuries of Spanish rule, a full half of Mexico's
wealth was in church hands! And church property, by law, could
not be taxed. Something had to give; the economic blood of
Mexico was being drained away.

The revolution of 1810, remember, was led by a priest
named Hidalgo. Another priest named Morelos carried it on.
This was a revolt against Spanish rule by churchmen who had
become Mexicanized.

The revolution of 1910, one century later, was not led by
priests but by men like Villa and Zapata, who went to church
only when it suited them. They fought, as Juárez did, against
the church.

Small wonder. The rich, fat church of Mexico had developed a bad habit of backing the wrong horse. The people rallied
behind the banners of Hidalgo and Morelos. But the church ex-
communicated them, then killed them.

The people supported Benito Juárez; the church backed
Maximilian against Juárez. You know what happened to Maximilian.

The church looked away when Díaz wiped out thousands
of Yaquis and sold Mexico's wealth to foreigners. The church
even supported the monster, Victoriano Huerta.

The people supported Madero and Obregón and Villa and Zapata.

It must have been hard, at times, for the church to oppose a popular hero like Benito Juárez. But Juárez, an Indian, once said that he would have welcomed Protestant missionaries to Mexico. Protestants, he said, might have taught the Indians to read instead of demanding that they spend their money on candles for the saints.

But the church in Mexico did establish schools. The University of Mexico was chartered in 1551, the first university in the western hemisphere. By 1821, when Spanish rule ended, there were 40 colleges and seminaries in Mexico.

Church education went all the way down to the primary level. Schools established by the Jesuits usually were the best. The schools, of course, prepared students to be good Catholics first, good Mexicans second.

It couldn't last. The people demanded change. In time, the politicians had to give it to them.

CHURCHES STRIKE!

Plutarco Calles succeeded Obregón as president of Mexico, then clamped down hard on the church in 1926.

He closed all religious schools, ordered all priests to register with the government and deported a batch of foreign priests and nuns.

Naturally, church leaders were outraged. Priests were forbidden to administer sacraments. In effect, the churches were closed and were to remain closed for three years. Mexico, the land of bells, suddenly went silent.

A terrible affair called the *Cristero* revolt broke out. Government schools were burned by the religious and *Cristero* bandits terrorized the central part of the country. *Cristeros* blew up a train running between Mexico City and Guadalajara. One hundred persons died. The government accused priests of leading the attack. This gave an excuse to the Calles generals to tear up the state of Jalisco, which was *Cristero* country. Sixty thousand Mexicans were herded into concentration camps.

Then a new U.S. ambassador, Dwight Morrow, worked his way into the conflict. He helped to end the *Cristero* revolt and open the churches again.

Never again would a Mexican government allow the church to grab and hold so much power and property.

So how did the ordinary Mexican feel about all this uproar? Well, ordinary Mexicans had little to do with bishops, so they were not terribly concerned. The peasants had their village churches and their Virgin of Guadalupe and their gaudy fiestas. All the rest was so much bureaucracy.

So it is today.

TWELVE
--- The Women

LOST IN THE MISTS OF MACHISMO

It took two hours to prepare a serving of corncakes for an Aztec family. Woman's work . . .

Aztec society was built on war, a simple, screaming, yelling kind of rock-and-spear war in which numbers were everything. Many died, and prisoners were either sacrificed or enslaved. So, the production of new human bodies was all-important. Woman's work . . .

While women bore children, found food and cooked it, their men fought, farmed and built temples. The dividing line was clear; not many women were brave or foolish enough to cross it.

So along came the Spanish, carrying with them the "civilized" culture of Europe. And did *El Conquistador*, Hernán Cortés, promptly liberate all of Mexico's women? Hah!

Remember Doña Marina, the young Indian woman? Cortés took up with her soon after landing in Mexico. But Cortés had a wife back in Cuba, Catalina. When the fighting in Mexico simmered down a bit, she joined her husband.

But, you say, what of Doña Marina? Ah . . .the clever Cortés had already married her off to one of his officers.

But Cortés and Catalina were not happy together. At a party, they had a loud argument. Cortés, it seems, suspected his wife of carrying on with one of her Indian servants.

On the morning after, Catalina's body was found in a well. She was quite dead. Rumor of the day: Cortés had strangled her, then stuffed her.

There was an investigation, of course. Verdict: asthma! Of course it was.

MOTHER-IN-LAW TROUBLE

Don Antonio de Mendoza, a great viceroy of Mexico, was a brilliant man and a strong leader. But he had mother-in-law trouble, just the same.

Doña María de Mendoza was a troublemaker, a constant burr under the viceroy's silver saddle. The viceroy and his mother-in-law fought like cats and dogs, in public and in private.

One day the viceroy went to the apartment of his mother-in-law and found her writing another nasty letter to the Council of the Indies. In the letter, she had again mentioned a few of the viceroy's faults. The viceroy grabbed the letter. Doña María grabbed it back. Angry words were spat by both.

Then the uproar was interrupted by the announcement that an archbishop, no less, waited to see the viceroy.

The viceroy came out, kissed the archbishop's ring, then excused himself.

Was that whimpering the archbishop heard? He went into the apartment of Doña María and found her sitting on the floor. Blood streamed from a gash on her forehead. Beside her lay a silver candlestick.

She survived, but she gave Viceroy Mendoza no more trouble.

Machismo is the word for it. *Machismo,* Indian style, Spanish style, Mexican style.

In the late 1890s, this picture was taken of Madame Candelaria Villanueva, of Mexican descent, who may have been the last living survivor of the siege of the Alamo.

What was it? Absolute control by the man of the house. The woman walks a step behind her husband. He rules the roost. She cooks, she bears children. He makes decisions; she goes along. The man proves his manliness by the number of his children; the woman wears herself out in bearing them, then again in caring for them.

It didn't end when the Spanish were finally thrown out in 1821. President Alvaro Obregón was the last of 18 children. His mother, you can be sure, didn't have time or energy to write many books or build many bridges.

ENTER MALINCHE

The first important woman to emerge from the mists of Mexican history was Malinche, Cortés's Doña Marina. A Nahua Indian by birth, she had been sold into slavery. When Cortés first met her, she was living as a slave among the Mayans. Since she spoke both Náhuatl, the Aztec language, and Mayan, she was a very important member of the Cortés party.

The Spanish conquest of Mexico, remember, succeeded only because the great *conquistador* got help from Indian enemies of the Aztecs. It was usually Malinche who talked to the Indians and convinced them that the god-man, Cortés, was unbeatable. More than once, a warning from Malinche of brewing trouble saved the party.

For a time, Malinche was also Cortés's mistress and bore him a son, Martín. Apparently this relationship ended when the wife of Cortés arrived from Cuba. A brave man but no fool, Cortés chose the moment to pass Malinche along to one of his lieutenants.

Could the Cortés expedition have succeeded without the brave, intelligent Indian woman? One can only guess. Certainly the task of Cortés would have been much more difficult without her. Since the fate of the reckless Spaniards hung by a hair more than once, Malinche might well have made the difference.

So, then, she is honored as a heroine of Mexico, right? Not by a long shot. Not in Mexico, at least. In fact, a *malinchista* is a traitor, one who sells out the homeland to foreigners. There are few monuments honoring Cortés in Mexico; there are even fewer honoring Malinche.

That really isn't fair. Malinche was no more traitor than were the thousands of Indians who fought on the side of Cortés. Those Indians, remember, had been ground under the Aztec heel for a long time. They would have joined up with the devil himself to knock over Moctezuma and his merry kidnappers.

And, of course, they didn't have to join up with the devil. When Cortés appeared, it seemed that they were joining up with Quetzalcóatl, the bearded god returning from the east. They knew nothing of Spain or the Spanish. It surely isn't fair to condemn Malinche and the Tlaxcalans because they helped weld Spanish chains which clamped down on Mexico for the next 300 years. Could Malinche have known that Spanish rule would result in near-extermination of Mexico's Indian population?

CHINA POBLANA

There was another slave woman who made her mark in Mexican history. The mark is nothing less than a national costume worn by women of Mexico on festive occasions. To the *gringo* tourist, the costume may look as Mexican as a tortilla.

But the woman who first wore the costume was Chinese! Or so the story goes . . .

Captured by slave traders in the Far East, the young woman was brought to Acapulco. There a wealthy man, Miguel Sosa, was attracted to her. He bought her, brought her to Puebla and gave her freedom.

Baptized as Catalina de San Juan, she began to help the poor. In time, *China Poblana,* or "Puebla China-girl," was known throughout Mexico for her good works. Her standard costume was a rough red skirt and white blouse.

The modern *China Poblana* costume is a bit fancier, of course. The white blouse is trimmed with embroidery; the red skirt has a green border and embroidered flowers. A delicate shawl tops the costume.

The remains of *China Poblana* rest in a great church in central Puebla. Her grave is marked with her Catholic name, Catalina de San Juan. Her bed and slippers are preserved in a state museum not far away.

WRITING LADY

Her mind was attracting attention at the age of eight. By 15, she was considered downright brilliant. Her name was Juana Inés de Asbaje y Ramírez Santillana.

She read widely; she wrote beautifully, mostly poetry. She was a good friend of the viceroy's wife, Doña Leonor Carreto, and took part in many of the great lady's social and literary activities. It especially delighted the viceroy to hear pretty little Juana, a mere slip of a girl, win arguments with pompous professors.

But she wanted to be more than a decoration of the viceroy's court. One day she took her books and her good mind to the convent of St. Jerome, taking the name "Sister Juana Inés de la Cruz."

For the next 25 years, she wrote and wrote. In time she came to be considered Mexico's best poet.

Full of surprises, Sister Juana one day gave away her books and stopped writing. Two years later, an epidemic swept through the convent. Juana devoted herself to nursing her sisters until she, too, became ill. She died on April 17, 1695. But she had made her mark and will be remembered.

WOMAN OF INDEPENDENCE

The *corregidor* of Querétaro, Don Miguel Domínguez, was disturbed. On this 14th day of September, 1810, news had come that the new viceroy had ordered the arrest of Father Hidalgo and other plotters against the rule of Spain. Don Miguel, chief administrator of the province, had good reason to be worried.

A city official accompanied by soldiers had brought the news. Sadly, the official reported that even Doña Josefa, the administrator's wife, was suspected!

Yes, the *corregidor* said, he would be glad to accompany the soldiers to the home of a certain Epigmenio González to search for guns and powder.

But first Don Miguel took the precaution of locking the door to the family quarters at the head of the stairs. (The Domínguez home was on the second floor, over some offices

A "faithful" copy of a self-portrait of Sister Juana, woman of
many talents.

and the jail.) Doña Josefa, affectionately known as *La Corregidora*, had heard the entire conversation through a floor vent. Now, finding herself locked in, she rapped three times on the floor with a broom handle.

Racing upstairs came the jailer, Ignacio Pérez. He, too, was a plotter. Through the keyhole, Doña Josefa gave Pérez his instructions.

"Go immediately to San Miguel," said *La Corregidora*. "Tell Captain Aldama that he must get word to Father Hidalgo and Captain Allende in Dolores. The lives of many persons, perhaps the fate of the nation, depend on you, Ignacio!"

Paul Revere Pérez did his job. You know the rest of the story. When Father Hidalgo got the warning early on the following morning, he decided to move immediately. The revolt against Spain had begun!

Hidalgo's revolt, as you know, was not successful. But his bold action set the stage for independence a decade later.

It didn't take long for Spanish authorities to discover that Don Miguel and Doña Josefa Domínguez were very much involved in the plot. There had been many meetings at their house, meetings attended by Hidalgo, Allende, Aldama and certainly by *La Corregidora*.

Don Miguel lost his job, but got off easy, by telling authorities all they wanted to know about his wife's activities. (It seems possible that she wanted it this way.)

La Corregidora, pregnant at the time, was imprisoned in a convent in Querétaro, than transferred to another convent in Mexico City. She was not released until 1814, when she rejoined her husband.

But it was not until the Spanish were finally kicked out in 1821 that *La Corregidora* was honored as a major maker of independence.

When she died in 1829, special services were held in most parts of the country. Her remains now rest under the Independence Column on Mexico City's main boulevard. Her stern, strong face looks out with seeming sadness from the Mexican five-*peso* and twenty-*peso* notes. She is one of very few women so honored in Mexico. Or anywhere, come to think of it.

THE WOMAN BEHIND MAXIMILIAN . . . PUSHING

Remember Carlota, the wife of Emperor Maximilian? Probably no woman in Mexican history had so much power in government as did Empress Carlota. The power was hers only as long as she controlled her husband but power it was, just the same.

Carlota, of course, was no more Mexican than her husband. She was a Belgian princess. Strong-willed and very ambitious for her beloved Maximilian, Carlota was a mover and a shaker during her short time in Mexico.

But such a sad ending was in store for both of them! There was a certain majesty in Maximilian's end before the firing squad on the Hill of Bells. But poor Carlota was fated to wander over Europe for years, without majesty or even dignity, until death released her from the demons in her mind.

Maximilian, you may remember, got into deep trouble when Napoleon III, ruler of France, decided to back off from his Mexican mistake. Without French troops behind him, Maximilian was out of the emperor business. Max had a notion that Napoleon was right; it was time for the emperor of Mexico to retreat to his castle, Miramar, on the Adriatic Sea.

Not Carlota. As usual, she provided most of her husband's backbone. Abdication, she said, was an act of cowardice. She would not allow Max to be a coward. So Carlota packed up and went to France. Napoleon MUST listen. The cause was not lost, she would argue. If Max could only have more time and more help . . .

It was a hard trip for Carlota. Just getting to Veracruz from Mexico City was tough enough. Terrible summer rains nearly washed her off the road. Then bandits stole the mules which pulled her carriage. Then, when she finally managed to reach France in August, Napoleon didn't want to see her; he complained of sickness.

Carlota insisted on seeing him, though. Three times she saw him, in fact. Each time she was disappointed. Becoming frantic, she left for Rome to see the Pope. Surely the Pope could make Napoleon see his mistake . . .

But the Pope didn't want to see her, either. When he did, finally, he had to listen to Carlota ramble on about her fear of

being poisoned. During her stay in Rome, she would drink only from public fountains. She was sure that Napoleon was trying to poison her.

Maximilian died on the Hill of Bells in 1867. Carlota was taken to Belgium. She never returned to Mexico. She died, a crazy old woman, in 1927.

Maximilian, who might have been willing to return to Europe if he could study butterflies, died in Mexico. You might say that he insisted upon it. After all, he had many chances to escape. Carlota loved Mexico and Mexicans and wanted to end her life there. But she died in Europe . . .

Just one more of history's tragic twists. It may sound like soap opera, but it really happened.

WOMEN OF BATTLE

The word was *soldadera*. Female soldier. In Mexican armies, there were many *soldaderas*. It was written: "In exhibitions of strength, endurance and courage, the *soldadera* was her man's equal, if she did not surpass him."

An army uniformed in silk stockings and dresses? It happened in the village of Puente de Ixtla. Widows, wives, daughters and sisters of Zapata soldiers organized their own battalion and went on wild raids through the Tetecala district. The leader was a tortilla maker called *La China*. With this husky woman showing the way, the female battalion terrorized the countryside to "avenge the dead."

Then there was Margarita Neri. She fought in the south with Zapata. It was said that she had been the mistress of a member of the Díaz cabinet.

Turned sour by the corruption of Díaz, the red-haired ex-dancer took to the hills. She formed her own group of bandits and announced her goal: she would personally cut off the head of Díaz. She fought well but didn't reach her goal. Díaz, you may remember, escaped with his head to Europe.

There was another woman of the south who had different feelings about Porfirio Díaz. Her name was Juana Cata Romero. When Díaz commanded the military garrison at Tehuantepec in the deep south, Juana Cata became his very good friend.

This engraving of Carlota seems to show a woman who knew what she wanted; those eyes mean business.

This young woman went riding off to revolution in 1916.

Juana liked to come to the barracks and play dice and billiards with the soldiers. The beautiful 28-year-old woman proved her loyalty by reporting all movements of enemy armies to Díaz. It is said that she signalled the right time for attacks by lighting bonfires on the river bank.

When Díaz became president, he didn't forget his good friends in Tehuantepec. Juana Cata Romero profited from his help but she may have gotten along all right without it. After a while, she owned the best stores in Tehuantepec, plus coconut and sugar plantations. (In 1904, her sugar won a prize at the St. Louis World's Fair.)

Under the Díaz regime, Doña Juana's power grew and grew. When a friend got into legal trouble, Doña Juana needed only to telegraph President Díaz, asking for a pardon. What Juana wanted, Juana got. She became the most powerful person in Tehuantepec.

A devout Catholic, Doña Juana built a chapel and schools. But, like many upper class Mexicans of her day, Doña Juana felt a powerful pull toward Europe. So, with the Díaz government riding high in the saddle, she left her wealth in the hands of a trusted friend and floated off to the Old World.

When she returned to Mexico, she had to wade through disaster. President Díaz had been kicked out and much of her wealth was gone. Her "trusted friend" and the revolutionaries had picked her clean.

Doña Juana wanted to die in her beloved Tehuantepec but didn't quite make it. More than 80 years old and ill, she left Mexico City for home. She died on the train taking her there.

The people of Tehuantepec still speak of her in a loving way. Doña Juana Cata Romero was a woman who made a deep mark on Mexican history.

OUT OF THE MISTS OF MACHISMO

Revolution in Mexico meant different things to different persons. To Father Hidalgo's followers, it meant kicking the Spaniards out. To the liberals who backed Juárez and Madero, it meant getting rid of dictators and returning to constitutional government. To Zapata's peons, it meant land reform.

Luz Corral, one of Pancho Villa's many widows, was still living in Chihuahua in the mid-1970s. Her home has been turned into a Villa museum---tourists most certainly welcome. The major exhibit is this old Dodge, which is said to be the one in which Villa died. Note bullet holes in rear of car.

To women, it meant a chance for new freedom.

In the early part of this century, most Mexican girls could expect a life of early marriage, then endless childbearing and housekeeping. No more, no less. After the revolution, change came, but slowly. It wasn't until the 1930s that women were admitted to Mexican universities. It wasn't until 1952 that all Mexican women could vote.

Mexico's women were in the world's spotlight in 1975. The United Nations chose Mexico City for its world conference of women, part of its International Women's Year. One hundred and thirty-three governments sent about 1300 delegates.

An important leader in the fight for women's rights in Mexico has been Amalia Ledón. As a young woman, she entered public life as the wife of the governor of Nayarit, a west coast state. When her husband died in 1935, Amalia Ledón entered public affairs on her own. She has been a member of the Mexican delegation to the United Nations. From 1948 to 1950, she worked as a vice-president of the World Commission of Women. Later she became Mexico's ambassador to Sweden and Finland, then to Austria and Switzerland. She crowned her career by being named Mexico's representative to the International Organization of Atomic Energy.

Out of the mists of *machismo* came Amalia Ledón. Her trail will be followed by many others.

THIRTEEN
--- *Modern Mexico*

CARDENAS SHOWS THE WAY

Remember Plutarco Calles? He was the president of Mexico who wanted to play musical chairs with Alvaro Obregón. First one would be president, then the other. They might have traded chairs for 30 years or so. Then Obregón was shot.

And Plutarco Calles had his chair pulled right out from under him . . .

Here's how it came about: Calles was elected in 1924, following Obregón's first term. Then, in 1928, it was Obregón's turn, but Obregón lived only three weeks after re-election. Calles couldn't just make himself president again without causing a great deal of nervousness, so he put in a puppet named Portes Gil. As the Big Boss, leader of the National Revolutionary Party, Calles held the puppet strings and really ran the country. It was said that when Calles spoke, no dog dared to bark.

Calles, who had started to be a reformer, turned into just another money-grubbing *caudillo*. Calles and his cronies had country houses in Cuernavaca, not far from Mexico City. Some

Mexicans called the neighborhood "The Street of the Forty Thieves."

In 1934, Big Boss chose another puppet. The name of this one, Lázaro Cárdenas, would haunt Plutarco Calles until his dying day.

The people of Mexico had never seen a presidential campaign like this one. The candidate could have stayed in Mexico City taking bows at banquets. Big Boss had spoken; the election was as good as won. But Lázaro Cárdenas, young and energetic, grabbed the opportunity to find out what was wrong with Mexico. He thought there was only one way to do that: talk to Mexicans. Radical idea!

So for months before the election, he travelled 29,000 kilometers by car, by train, by mule and on foot. He spoke to large gatherings in the towns and cities but he also wandered off into the countryside. Cárdenas asked questions and he listened. Mostly he listened.

By election time, the plain people of Mexico felt they really knew Lázaro Cárdenas. They had talked to him; perhaps they had even touched him. Not even the great man of the people, Benito Juárez, had been able to reach out as Cárdenas had.

On election day, he won 98 per cent of the vote. Then, with the people solidly behind him, he began to move.

Calles and his friends had grown rich from the profits of illegal gambling houses; Cárdenas began to shut them down. Calles had slowed down distribution of land to the peasants; Cárdenas speeded it up. When workers went on strike, Cárdenas did not beat them down with soldiers; he expressed sympathy.

Increasingly nervous as his "puppet" jerked the strings, Calles tried to stir Catholics to rebellion. This had worked before; it didn't work this time. Cárdenas had let the church forces know that anti-church laws might be relaxed if they behaved themselves.

Before long, state governors appointed by Calles were being bounced from their jobs. The bandwagon was rolling for Cárdenas; the Calles crowd was beginning to leap aboard.

Calles decided it was time to take control, so he moved back to Mexico City. But there he found that his house was under guard. There was little for the Big Boss to do but play golf, which he did.

But Calles in the capital was like a fox in a chickenhouse; either the fox had to leave or feathers would fly. When labor unions began to cry out for the death of the former *caudillo*, President Cárdenas took pity, flew Calles to California and dumped him there.

Every time Calles had attacked, Cárdenas had beaten him to the punch. Within two years after taking office, the young president had wiped out a dictatorship and put the revolution back on track. And, wonder of wonders in Mexico, it had all been done without bloodshed!

How? First, Cárdenas had listened to the people. Even after becoming president, he listened. He set up a system by which any Mexican, during a certain hour each day, could telegraph the president without cost. If the natives were restless, Cárdenas wanted to know it.

Also, Cárdenas knew better than to ask Mexicans to tighten their belts while he was getting fat. After becoming president, Cárdenas chose not to live in magnificent Chapultepec Castle. Then he cut his own salary in half! It had been customary for the president's wife to receive an entertainment allowance. Cárdenas had it stopped. (We'll assume he asked his wife's permission for this bold act.)

Campesinos and laborers came to the presidential palace by the thousands. Cárdenas listened to them, while leaving politicians and generals and businessmen waiting outside.

Cárdenas had been a general but he laid aside his soldier suit. He was inaugurated as president wearing plain business clothes. He worked in the same clothes.

It had been customary to welcome the arrival of the president at the palace with a bugle fanfare. Cárdenas cut that out. It had been the custom to hang portraits of the president in public buildings. Cárdenas cut that out, too.

CARDENAS TO THE RESCUE

Soon a joke about Cárdenas was making the rounds. It was said that one morning his secretary laid two pieces of paper on his desk: a list of important matters and a telegram.

Lázaro Cárdenas was one of Mexico's greatest presidents. He knew what the people needed and wanted because he took the trouble to listen to them. He went to them; they came to him.

First item on the list: Bank reserves very low.
Cárdenas said, "Tell the treasurer."
Second item: Farm production dropping.
Cárdenas said, "Tell the minister of agriculture."
Third item: Important message from Washington.
Cárdenas said, "Tell foreign affairs."

He opened the telegram, which read: MY CORN DRIED, MY BURRO DIED, MY SOW WAS STOLEN, MY BABY IS SICK. SIGNED, PEDRO JUAN, VILLAGE OF TENANCINGO.

Cárdenas said, "Order the presidential train at once. I must go to Tenancingo."

The people had their free telegraph line for sending messages to the president. The president, by his acts, was sending signals back. "You can trust me," he was saying.

And trust him they did.

A remarkable man, was Lázaro Cárdenas. He had also been a remarkable child.

The year 1910, you may remember, was when the regime of Porfirio Díaz was challenged by Francisco Madero. It was also the year in which a 15-year-old boy went to work in the tax collector's office in the village of Jiquilpan, state of Michoacán. Since the office of jailer was open, the boy took that job, too. Too young to be jailer, you say?

Not this boy. His name was Lázaro Cárdenas.

At 18, he decided to become a soldier. Victoriano Huerta was president of Mexico at the time; young Lázaro saw him as the monster he was. Soon after joining the guerrilla army of General García Aragón, Cárdenas was named paymaster. In a guerrilla army, this meant that he guarded and divided the loot. Already Cárdenas was being noticed as a man who could be trusted to handle other people's money.

For 12 years, Cárdenas stayed in the army. With the Carranza forces fighting Pancho Villa, Cárdenas was noticed by The Man --- General Plutarco Elías Calles. In 1920, Cárdenas was promoted to general. Calles probably arranged it. It didn't seem to matter that Cárdenas was only 25 years old. (Calles called him *El Chamaco* --- The Kid.)

The young general didn't tarnish his brass. Once he was given one million *pesos* for a military campaign. He finished the job successfully, then turned back 700,000 *pesos* to the treasury. Fantastic! Three other generals involved in the same campaign and given the same amount of money, turned back nothing.

While Cárdenas was commander at Tampico, then center of the oil industry, he was offered a new car by the local bigwigs. His own car was a junker, but he refused the gift. In the back of his mind, he stored away the knowledge of how the oil business operated.

Mexican generals had earned a reputation for brutality. More than once, Cárdenas refused to live up to the reputation. When he found himself in a position where he could easily wipe out his enemy, the young general instead walked alone into the enemy camp.

"Give up." said Cárdenas. "I don't want to kill you." Luckily for Cárdenas, the enemy saw it his way.

Most generals took prisoners, then shot them. Cárdenas refused to do this.

He became governor of his home state of Michoacán. The lessons he learned would serve him well when he became president of Mexico.

His first term as governor ended; his new job was commander of the military zone at Puebla. He went there with his new wife, Amalia Solórzano. Now, think of this: Cárdenas was a general and had been a state governor. Two easy ways to get rich, right?

But Cárdenas, moving to Puebla, had to borrow money to pay for the hauling of his furniture! An incredible man . . .

Cárdenas was rising. His big opportunity came when Calles backed him for president. The Big Boss thought that Lázaro Cárdenas in the president's chair would be a different person from Lázaro Cárdenas in the soldier suit.

He wasn't. He was the same honest Mexican.

➡

In 1943, a farmer in the state of Michoacán saw steam rising from his cornfield. Then hot lava began to ooze from the earth. In a relatively short time, the volcano cone now called Paracutín was formed. Here we see the crater with steam still rising. Yes, that is a church steeple at right, jutting from the lava. The eruption buried two villages and forced 4000 persons to leave their homes.

UPROAR IN THE OIL FIELDS

Cárdenas would need all of his public support during a crisis in 1938. For many years, foreign-owned oil companies had operated in Mexico. Most owners were English and American. They paid low wages and took their profits out of Mexico. They even had the gall to charge more for their oil in Mexico than in other countries! Their bad habits had been learned during the regime of Porfirio Díaz. They didn't realize soon enough that a different kind of president was running Mexico.

After a labor dispute in which the owners defied a Supreme Court ruling, President Cárdenas took the bold step: he went on national radio to announce that the oil officials were being sent out of the country and their properties would be taken over by the government.

What an uproar! The British yelled so loudly that Cárdenas broke off diplomatic relations with Great Britain.

Although American business interests called Cárdenas a Communist and worse, U.S. President Franklin D. Roosevelt took a different line. Mexico had a right, he said, to take over the oil property. But, he warned, the companies should be paid. In time, they were.

For a few years after the oil properties had been taken over, the country had a hard time. Mexicans had to learn how to operate the oil field machinery. Until they did, no money came in. But the country rallied behind its bold leader; those who could, loaned money to the national treasury. The crisis passed.

It was a proud moment. At last Mexican oil would be used to benefit Mexicans. The national oil company was *Petróleos Mexicanos.* Now it is usually referred to as "Pemex." Pemex is the largest single employer in the country.

The best may be yet to come. In the early 1970s, the world's oil barons pricked up their ears at rumors coming out of Mexico. Mexican oil scientists had found fields even richer than those in Alaska!

And because of the bold action of Lázaro Cárdenas in 1938, profits from these discoveries would stay in Mexico.

The eagle and the serpent properly perch on the marble case containing the Constitution of Mexico, on view in the Gallery of Mexican History, Mexico City.

During his six years in office, Cárdenas spent about one-third of his time travelling and talking to the people. You may say, "Fine, but who was tending the store in Mexico City?"

Tending the store were the honest, capable persons the president had chosen. Nobody walked off with the light fixtures in the National Palace while Cárdenas was president.

Mexican presidents had long talked of land reform; Cárdenas actually did it. During his term of office, 18,000 hectares (about 45 million acres) of land were distributed to peasants. This was more than twice the total of all previous governments combined!

In 1940, Cárdenas retired to country life in Michoacán. Two years later, he was called back to national service. Mexico had declared war on Germany. President Avila Camacho chose Cárdenas to command the Pacific defense zone. After the war, Cárdenas again retired to Michoacán. He died there in 1970.

Like any country, Mexico has had its share of presidents who were thieves, bunglers or brutes. Or all three.

But in the last century, Mexico had Benito Juárez.

In this century, it had Lázaro Cárdenas.

Looking back, these two seem to make up for most of the others.

In April, 1943, a historic event occurred in Monterrey, Mexico. President Roosevelt of the U.S. had gone there for a meeting with President Camacho of Mexico.

So why is this historic? Because a U.S. president had never before visited Mexico! It took a world war to bring it about.

Since those days, Mexico and the U.S. have grown closer together. It had to happen. The two countries share about 3200 kilometers of unfortified border. The wars between them are in the past. The scars remain but the bloodshed is done with. Now the two countries share some common ground and, just possibly, a common destiny.

By the Treaty of Guadalupe Hidalgo in 1848, a chunk of land as large as present-day Mexico was "sold" to the *gringos*. That land now makes up most of the southwestern U.S.

Along with the land came at least 75,000 Mexicans, citizens of Mexico who happened to live on the ground that was sold. The first "Chicanos" didn't move to the U.S., nor were they born in the U.S. The U.S. moved to them.

In modern times, things have changed. The Mexican community in and around Los Angeles, California, is the third largest concentration of persons of Mexican descent in the world. Only Mexico City and Guadalajara are larger . . . and some head counters are not so sure about Guadalajara.

Five states (California, Texas, Arizona, New Mexico and Colorado) have the heaviest populations of Mexican-Americans and Mexicans. Mexican-Americans, sure, but MEXICANS? Most certainly; millions of them. Many came as farm workers under the *bracero* program and stayed. Some came as tourists . . . and stayed. Some came as "wetbacks,"wading across the Rio Grande River . . . and stayed.

Between 1900 and 1930, one-tenth of the total population of Mexico entered the U.S.!

The most famous Mexican-American is Cesar Chávez, leader of the United Farm Workers. The U.F.W. was the first successful farm workers' union in this country.

Food production in the U.S., considered nothing less than a miracle by the rest of the world, depends heavily on the work of persons of Mexican descent. Some are U.S. citizens; some are Mexican citizens, with legal work permits; many others are illegal.

They are illegal but they are here. They are not citizens, but they are here. The U.S. Immigration Service regularly sends thousands of them back to Mexico but they return as soon as they can.

U.S. Immigration says that there might be as many as 12 million illegal Mexicans in the U.S. Nobody knows for sure. So where do the U.S. and Mexico go from here? The two countries share not only 3200 kilometers of border; they share experiences and traditions ranging from Lincoln and Juárez to the Alamo and tacos. What once was a great part of Mexico is now part of the U.S., sold by a Mexican president through the Treaty of Guadalupe Hidalgo. It happened; no one can turn back the clock.

Children, children, children---Mexico's glory and Mexico's burden.
These were photographed north of Oaxaca on a school outing.
Note teacher with bullhorn at left. The group was 10 times larger
than the camera could handle---or the teacher.

Mexican President Luis Echeverría, who ended his term in 1976, said that the promise of Mexico would be fulfilled only when Mexicans didn't have to leave their homeland to make a living.

Between 1950 and 1975, Mexico's population leaped from 30 million to 60 million. Very few countries in the world have had to cope with such an explosion of people. Experts predict that by the year 2000, the country's population will have doubled again!

Food production has gone up, but still Mexico cannot feed itself. Sixty million more mouths to feed in 25 years . . .

The Mexican government has built tens of thousands of new housing units, but the grim slums of Mexico City remain. Sixty million more persons to house in 25 years . . .

For the last quarter century, Mexico has been the most prosperous and progressive country in Latin America. Yet the flow of Mexicans to the U.S. threatens to become a flood. Sixty million more in 25 years . . .

Out of the century of bloodshed that was Mexican politics between 1810 and 1910, there has flowered a stable government. Not a perfect government, by any means; not a truly democratic government, but a government that lifts its head toward the goals of Juárez and Cárdenas and condemns the crimes of Santa Anna and Huerta.

But still they flow north, hiding in cars and trucks, wading the rivers at night, being caught by U.S. immigration officers and sent back, only to return again and again . . .

Tourists from the U.S. have flocked to Mexico for years. Tourism has been Mexico's major industry; most of the tourists are *gringos*. What draws them south? The great beauty of the sun-splashed Mexican land, the stunning historical sites, the warm welcome of the smiling Mexican people.

And Mexicans flow north, usually for different reasons. But the exchange goes on, Mexican and *gringo*, and it will go on, because the surge of history can't be stopped. Mexico and the U.S. are linked forever, like it or not.

The border has been marked in blood, stained with fear and tragedy. In the best of all possible worlds, it will be marked with patience and understanding and love. Especially patience . . .

The *gringo* says, "Good luck."

The Mexican says, *"Buena suerte."*

➡

This legend decorates the entrance foyer of one of the world's finest museums, Museum of Anthropology in Chapultepec Park, Mexico City.

NFIANZA ANTE EL PORVENI
GRANDEZA DE SU PASAD

ESPEJO DE ESA GRANDEZ

UNIDAD DEL DESTINO HUMAN

LOS HOMBRES QUEDARA SIEMPR
S HAYAN LUCHADO PARA ERIGIRLA

SELECTED BIBLIOGRAPHY

Alba, Victor; THE MEXICANS: THE MAKING OF A NATION; Frederick A. Praeger; 1967.

Atkin, Ronald; REVOLUTION! MEXICO 1910 - 1920; The John Day Co.; 1970.

Beals, Carleton; HOUSE IN MEXICO; Hastings House; 1958.

Beals, Carleton; MEXICAN MAZE; J. B. Lippincott Co.; 1931.

Bloomgarden, Richard; THE EASY GUIDE TO MEXICO CITY; Litográfica Turmex, S.A.; 1967.

Bloomgarden, Richard; THE EASY GUIDE TO PUEBLA AND CHOLULA; Litográfica Turmex, S.A.; 1973.

Brenner, Anita; THE WIND THAT SWEPT MEXICO; University of Texas Press; 1971.

Carpenter, Frank G.; MEXICO; Doubleday, Page & Co.; 1924.

Casasola, Gustavo; HISTORIA GRAFICA DE LA REVOLUCION MEXICANA 1900 - 1970; Editorial Trillas; 1973.

Miguel Covarrubias; MEXICO SOUTH; Alfred A. Knopf; 1946.

Díaz del Castillo, Bernal; A. P. Maudslay, translator; THE DISCOVERY AND CONQUEST OF MEXICO 1517 - 1521; Farrar, Straus and Giroux; 1956.

ENCYCLOPAEDIA BRITTANICA; Encyclopaedia Brittanica, Inc.; 1973.

Foley, Charles; "Before Columbus," ILLUSTRATED LONDON NEWS; Nov. 1974.

Franck, Harry A.; TRAILING CORTEZ THROUGH MEXICO; Grosset & Dunlap; 1935.

Garrett, W. E.; "South to Mexico City," NATIONAL GEOGRAPHIC MAGAZINE; August 1968.

Garvin, Richard M.; THE CRYSTAL SKULL; Doubleday & Company, Inc.; 1973.

de la Haba, Louis; "Mexico, the City That Founded a Nation," NATIONAL GEOGRAPHIC MAGAZINE; May 1973.

Hamill, Hugh M., Jr.; THE HIDALGO REVOLT; University of Florida Press; 1966.

Haslip, Joan; THE CROWN OF MEXICO; Holt, Rinehart and Winston; 1971.

Johnson, William Weber; LIFE WORLD LIBRARY: MEXICO; Time Incorporated; 1966.

Leonard, Jonathan Norton; ANCIENT AMERICA; Time Incorporated; 1967.

McWilliams, Carey; THE MEXICANS IN AMERICA; Teachers College Press; 1968.

Meier, Matt S. and Feliciano Rivera; THE CHICANOS: A HISTORY OF MEXICAN AMERICANS; Hill and Wang; 1972.

MEXICO AND CENTRAL AMERICA; American Automobile Association; 1971, 1977.

Miller, Merle; PLAIN SPEAKING; Berkley Publishing Corporation; 1974.

Nevin, David; THE OLD WEST: THE TEXANS; Time - Life Books; 1975.

"A New Shrine for the Brown Virgin," TIME; Dec. 20, 1976.

Newlon, Clarke; FAMOUS MEXICAN - AMERICANS; Dodd, Mead & Co.; 1972.

Norman, James; TERRY'S GUIDE TO MEXICO, Doubleday & Co., Inc.; 1972.

Oates, Stephen B., General Editor; THE REPUBLIC OF TEXAS; American West Publishing Co.; 1968.

O'Shaughnessy, Edith; A DIPLOMAT'S WIFE IN MEXICO; Harper & Brothers Publishers; 1916.

Pagden, A. R., translator and editor; HERNAN CORTES: LETTERS FROM MEXICO; Grossman Publishers; 1971.

Parkes, Henry Bamford; A HISTORY OF MEXICO; Houghton Mifflin; 1969.

Payne, Robert; MEXICO CITY; Harcourt, Brace and World Inc.; 1968.

Rosenblum, Morris; HEROES OF MEXICO; Fleet Press Corporation; 1969.

Simpson, Lesley Byrd; MANY MEXICOS; University of California Press; 1966.

Smith, Bradley; MEXICO: A HISTORY IN ART; Doubleday & Co., Inc.; 1968.

von Hagen, Victor W.; THE AZTEC: MAN AND TRIBE; The New American Library; 1958.

Weisberger, Bernard A.; THE IMPACT OF OUR PAST; American Heritage Publishing Co., Inc.; 1972.

Wolf, Eric R.; SONS OF THE SHAKING EARTH; University of Chicago Press; 1959.

Womack, John, Jr.; ZAPATA AND THE MEXICAN REVOLUTION; Random House Vintage Books; 1970.

YEARBOOK 1975; Facts on File; 1975.

316

ABOUT THOSE OTHER BOOKS . . .

It takes more than a bibliography to do justice to the printed matter spawned by the wild and wonderful history of Mexico. So here's a sampler:

THE WORLD OF THE AZTECS by William H. Prescott (Tudor Publishing Co., New York) is brisk, readable and heavily illustrated.

A large and handsome volume, THE NATIONAL MUSEUM OF ANTHROPOLOGY, MEXICO, by Pedro Ramírez Vázquez and others, is a stunner published by Harry N. Abrams, Inc., New York. This lavishly illustrated coffee table object attempts to portray in pictures one of the world's finest museums and comes as close to succeeding as any book could.

Those who can't get enough of pre-Columbian art should sample MEXICO: A HISTORY IN ART by Bradley Smith (Doubleday & Co., New York). This is another big one with delights for the eyes on almost every page.

Do you want to know how it really was during the amazing Spanish conquest of Mexico? Then read it as it was written by a sweating soldier in the ranks of Cortés, Bernal Díaz del Castillo. He fought, bled, suffered and, at last, as an old man, wrote about the incredible experience, which was surely one of the most remarkable of human history. Read all about it in THE DISCOVERY AND CONQUEST OF MEXICO by Bernal Díaz del Castillo (Farrar, Straus and Giroux) and blow your mind.

If you liked the soldier's story, you might be ready for the account of the glorious leader. Try HERNAN CORTES: LETTERS FROM MEXICO (Grossman Publishers, New York).

The story of Emperor Maximilian and Empress Carlota in Mexico couldn't be real; it had to be a plot for a spectacular movie. But it was real; it was also a movie. Read THE CROWN OF MEXICO by Joan Haslip (Holt, Rinehart and Winston, Inc. and Avon). Had he lived so long, Shakespeare would have stolen the plot.

For more about the explosive revolution years, try ZAPATA AND THE MEXICAN REVOLUTION by John Womack, Jr. (Knopf and Random House, New York) and REVOLUTION! by

Ronald Atkin (The John Day Co., New York). Both are wild stuff.

Texans might want to read THE REPUBLIC OF TEXAS, published by American West Publishing Co., Palo Alto, California. Its old maps are fascinating.

Californians can get a feast of information about the Spanish adventure in California from THE SPANISH WEST, published by Time-Life Books, New York. The illustrations are outstanding, as one expects from Time-Life.

For more on modern Mexico, try Time-Life's MEXICO CITY, one of The Great Cities series. Or MEXICO, published by Lane Magazine & Book Co., Menlo Park, California. Or MEXICO from the Life World Library series published by Time Incorporated, New York. All three hit hard with strong photographs.

INDEX TO PERSONS AND PLACES

320

321